Praise for *BRAND YOURSELF*

'If you want to move mountains in your life, your personal brand had better stand for something special. This book is great whether you already are a successful leader or wish to become one.'

Raymond Aaron
New York Times Top Ten Bestselling Author
www.aaron.com

'Rachel Quilty has decisively moved the personal branding discipline forward. Her work is leading edge, informative, inspiring, challenging and a must read for anyone who wants greater influence and success.'

Scott Letourneau
CEO – Nevada Corporate Planners, Inc.
www.nvinc.com

'Nothing will pay greater dividends than building a personal brand. Rachel Quilty's Brand Yourself book is a great way to start your own personal branding process.'

Ann Reinten
Image Innovators
www.imageinnovators.com

'When it comes to branding and creating your celebrity image, there is no better Expert on the subject than Rachel Quilty of the Jump The Q. Rachel's professionalism, quality, and attention to detail is exemplary. She not only walks the talk, but gets the result for her clients and her students worldwide in terms of brand recognition. It is my pleasure to recommend her book to you if you are looking to go to the next level with your Personal Brand to achieve greater success.'

Debra Thompson Roedl
CEO – Wealth Alliance Group
www.debrathompsonroedl.com.

'Rachel Quilty's Brand Yourself book is an invaluable source of inspiration and guidance in my business which relies heavily on personal branding. I cannot recommend it highly enough for every direct sales agent, out there! This is a must-have resource for everyone in direct sales. This insightful and instructional book on personal branding will help you create a competitive edge and position your personal brand to stand out from the crowd.'

Marina Hirst
Direct Sales Consultant – Intimo

'Rachel Quilty's thorough and systematic approach to designing and positioning your brand will prove useful anyone who wishes to stand out in the market place. Read Brand Yourself and learn the secrets from Rachel Quilty, the Authority on personal branding.'

Trish Jenkins
Author/Speaker – Dangerous Wealth
www.dangerouswealthsecrets.com

'Your clients believe in you and are proud to support your business when your personal style and personal brand are consistent. Rachel Quilty gives you the practical 'how-to' for creating a personal brand that is authentic and attractive to your clients and allows you to live and work in flow.'

Narelle Todd,
Director – Successful Living Pty Ltd
www.successfulliving.com.au

BRAND
YOURSELF

BRAND
YOURSELF

**HOW TO DESIGN, BUILD AND POSITION
YOUR PERSONAL BRAND**

Rachel Quilty: 'The Authority' in Personal Branding.

First edition 2010

National Library of Australia Cataloguing-in-Publication entry:

Quilty, Rachel
Brand Yourself: how to design and build a powerful persuasive personal brand

1st ed.

ISBN: 978 1 921630 44 6 (pbk.)

    1. Branding (Marketing) Brand name products.
    2. Imagery (Psychology) Product management.
    3. Marketing—Management.
    4. Success in business.

658.827

Published by Global Publishing Group
PO Box 517, Mt. Evelyn, Victoria 3796, Australia
Email: info@globalpublishinggroup.com.au

For further information about orders:
Phone: +61 3 9736 1156
Email: info@GlobalPublishingGroup.com.au
Website: www.GlobalPublishingGroup.com.au

A Love Story ...

Some people hear the knocking of their dreams
and never answer the door.
Some people tentatively open the door but close it,
the risk seeming too great.
Some people, despite their fears,
answer the knocking door of their heart.

Those who follow their heart, despite their fear, are the brave.
To do what they love, they are the warriors in modern times.
Courage is, defined as taking action despite fear.

This book is dedicated to ...

My husband ... Michael Quilty
You are my warrior.
You are courageous.
I love you so much.
I am so proud of you.
And I will always love you.

— Rachel

Special Acknowledgements

Many warm thanks to:

Darren Stephens, the marketing mastermind behind *Men are from Mars*. And the CEO the Global Publishing Group who encouraged me to write this book.

Andrew and Daryl Grant, Our Internet Secrets.
My millionaire mentors who told me to get on with the book already.

Debra Roedl Thompson, Wealth Alliance Group.
My business empire strategist who shared my Expert Empire vision.

My friends: **Julie O'Donovan, Lynelle Hills, Narelle Todd & Eva H.**

Dream Centre, Gold Coast, Australia - the best Church in the world.

And **Monique, Mum and Nana**.
The strong, independent and intelligent women I love so much.

Contents

Author's Note

Hi, I'm Rachel Quilty, your Personal Brand Strategist from Jump the Q® and my goal is to help you design your personal brand, identify strategies to build your professional profile, and assist you to leverage your personal brand to become the authority in your industry.

My strength and expertise is in defining and designing your true personal brand. This book will help you unearth the real you, your purpose and your mission. My role is to nurture dreams of success. Like a movie director, I nurture your brand creation with you in the starring role.

The following quote captures the essence of a great personal brand.
> "You look famous, are legendary, appear complex, act easy, radiate presence, travel light, seem a dream, and finally, prove real."

Congratulations on wanting to be that person.

This book is about discovering, defining and creating a captivating and compelling personal brand. Your personal brand!

It involves you taking center stage in your own success. After all as they say, "Life isn't a dress rehearsal."

So, now it's your turn ...

Scene 1. Take 1. *Action!*

Foreword

When it comes to branding, most people associate it with products derived from large corporations, when in fact branding starts with *You* first and is everything from your personal signature style to your business image and then the products and services you represent. You have to think of yourself and 'brand yourself' as a celebrity within your own right. Celebrities don't enter the spotlight by accident and neither should you.

The goal with most celebrity brand marketing campaigns is to stand out and become memorable in the public's eye by creating an image of success, power and popularity that greatly enhances their earning potential and longevity in the market. And, just as with celebrities, it is important that you are strategic about your personal brand and image by creating it and managing it to achieve the same goals.

As Rachel has stated here in *Brand Yourself* ... 'the better your brand, the better your bottom line.' The step-by-step strategies that are presented herein are clear-cut principles. If you learn the principles and apply the knowledge you will greatly increase your both your personal bottom line and your business bottom line as well as your longevity in the market. Either way you have the win-win solution with Brand Yourself to start your journey today.

Debra Thompson Roedl
Wealth Alliance Group International
www.WealthAllianceGroup.com
'We Turn Your Expertise Into Wealth!'

Introduction: Brand Yourself for Success...

Congratulations! Simply by making the decision to build your personal brand is an impressive decision.

You see ... personal branding is by far the most powerful success and business building tool ever devised. So, get ready to stake your claim as the authority in your industry and position your brand as the only choice brand.

Consider this ... would you like a persuasive and powerful personal brand? If you said 'Yes!!', then you're in the right place. This book really is a step-by-step instructional manual on building a powerful and compelling personal brand so that you can achieve your wildest dreams.

So, let's start by doing a quick overview of this Brand Yourself book. It covers how to:

- determine what personal branding really is
- discover why branding yourself is essential for your survival
- learn the principles of positioning yourself as the authority
- brand yourself in ten easy action steps
- develop a Brand Yourself Action Plan for your success

Now ... our objective here is for you to identify how you can:

- build a powerful personal brand
- create a brand that attracts clients
- develop a personal brand that reflects your potential and goals
- premium price yourself through differentiation
- brand yourself as the industry leader

This book really is an instructional manual on discovering, defining and designing your best personal brand. You'll find there are many areas where you are required to answer questions, complete various assignments and develop a number of plans for your personal brand.

Essentially, choosing to build your personal branding is like stepping off a cliff. You have become fully committed to the action you have taken.

Well done on investing in yourself.

Your first assignment is simply to identify some famous personal brands you may have heard of and that appeal to you.

You may list the likes of:
Donald Trump
Oprah
Paris Hilton
Madonna
Tiger Woods
Barrack Obama
Warren Buffet
Martin Luther King
Steve Irwin
David and Victoria Beckham
Elton John
Richard Branson
Princess Diana
Lady Gaga
Nelson Mandela
Jesus Christ
Mother Teresa
Gandhi

As you can see, the list is endless.

My personal objective and commitment to you is to assist you to position your personal brand as the authority in your industry and develop a **Brand Yourself Action Plan** to achieve this. In fact, we provide you with the resources you need to build an *Oprah Winfrey* or *Richard Branson* brand.

After all '*in the future everybody will be world famous for fifteen minutes.*' Will you be ready for your *Andy Warhol's* promise of fifteen minutes of fame? Are you excited about the opportunities that will undoubtedly come your way?

To measurably improve your professional image, personal brand and brand equity, get your FREE Quick Start Guide — **Brand Yourself Blueprint** at www.brandyourselfblueprint.com

In this book, I include a number of quotes from many famous personal brands which you may recognize. Often they speak more eloquently on the topic. I encourage everyone to identify with an idol and model their success.

For example, in the book, *Oprah Speaks*, the author adds 'Oprah's star status didn't just land in her lap. A daunting work ethic, excellent time management, amazing business acumen, and a massive dose of showmanship made her the number 1 talk show host worldwide. She's a very important brand in our culture. Her presence as a brand is embodied by trust, human-to-human connections and realness. Her audience has come to believe Oprah is real and she is telling the truth.' You may wish to model Oprah and her attributes.

This Brand Yourself book assists you to identify the foundational blocks to building your personal brand and positioning you as the authority in your industry or field. It is an incredible resource for assessing your existing personal brand and identifying how to re-position your personal brand to create momentum.

In fact, your personal brand affects everything ... including your:

- marketability
- market position
- market penetration
- ability to attract and keep clients
- the prices clients are willing to pay for your products and services

There are really only four steps to improving your personal and business brand.

Step 1.   Identify your existing brand

Step 2.   Determine your preferred brand

Step 3.   Plan the strategic aspects of your new brand

Step 4.   Implement your new brand

However, in saying that... to make the process logical and simple, we have developed a ten step **Brand Yourself Action Plan.**™

The ten **Brand Yourself Action Steps** to build a persuasive personal brand and dominate your marketplace are:

Action Step 1.   Discover your existing personal brand

Action Step 2.   Determine your brand's target audience

Action Step 3.   Define your true personal brand

Action Step 4.   Dominate your market as the authority

Action Step 5.   Design your unique personal brand

Action Step 6.   Develop your brand's signature style

Action Step 7.   Devise your personal brand marketing plan

Action Step 8.   Decide your desired outcomes, resources and skill set

Action Step 9.   Deploy your personal brand message

Action Step 10. Deliver your personal brand promise

When you strategically manage expectations of your personal brand through your deliberate attributes, actions and non actions, you become a compelling and captivating personal brand. Therefore, the goal is for you to be known entirely for who you are as a person and what you stand for.

We intentionally use the term 'the Authority' not 'an authority'. Anyone can become an authority on a subject. Our goal is to create your personal brand as the 'only choice' brand – 'the Authority'. Now, when you develop your **Brand Yourself Action Plan** through this filter or with this distinction in mind, it can promote subtle adjustments that will distinguish and differentiate your brand.

Don't underrate or underestimate this distinction!

It is important to review and create your branding through this 'the Authority' filter and position your personal brand as 'THE' authority.

The principles of positioning yourself as the **AUTHORITY** in your industry are:

A = Attributes
U = Unique
T = Territory
H = Hook
O = Opportunity
R = Reliability
I = Image
T = Trustworthy
Y = Yourself

And more importantly, if you don't brand yourself, someone else will.

This book gives you the tools to brand yourself before someone else does it to you – or to change your brand if it doesn't reflect your true self. This book gives you control over how you're perceived.

Does your personal brand have momentum?

Consider Jump the Q®s Momentum Formulae for Success below. What areas are unclear within your personal brand? Seems so simple doesn't it ... but how many people honestly take the time to clarify the specifics exactly?

This is the secret to your personal brand momentum. Often people engage our services to assist them with the 'how to' build awareness of their personal brand without really fully considering the:

- Who
- What
- Where
- When
- Why
- What if

For over fifteen years, I have been researching and providing personal branding services. This in depth book is an accumulation of ideas and concepts that I have tried and tested over this time and which may work for you. Although, you will recognize that what works for you may not work for others.

In fact within our personal branding consultation, no two consultations are ever the same. One question may promote a wave of responses and another nothing. Do not worry about this happening. Just allow your mind time to process the questions and provide a response. It will happen.

You will notice that we reinforce some concepts by repeating them as they apply to the various Action Steps. This is because the principles may apply to more than one Action Step and hence may be repeated. This has been done intentionally to reiterate and highlight their importance and continued application.

This book introduces you to a number of business concepts which have been adjusted to a personal brand context as opposed to a broader business context.

For example, we are familiar with the necessity to undertake accounting or procedural audits; within this book we consider your personal brand audit. Without an awareness of your existing brand and what image would ideally support your brand in the eyes of your clients, the more advanced action steps to position yourself for success and command your future are difficult. Consistently within a business you cannot make sustainable inroads without first conducting a comprehensive SWOTT to determine the company's current strengths and weaknesses.

You can read this book in conjunction with the **Brand Yourself Action Plan** and Action Plan Work Journal.

See www.brandyourselfactionplan.com for more information.

I recommend transcribing each section into your Action Plan Work Journal so that you can continue to monitor your brand's progress and your professional growth.

While we have included a number of case studies, you will see that the number we could have included is huge. As a result, we have elected to focus on the development of your brand as our primary focus. We include work journals, case studies, video training and reference manuals in our online programs to illustrate and expand on each of the areas of your personal brand. See our Brand Yourself Resources section for further information.

Branding combines concepts that you've heard time and time again. If you are familiar with some of the content – look for the distinctions. If you think to yourself yes I know that, immediately ask yourself if you are doing it. If the answer is no, ask yourself why not. Ask yourself what you should work on next to lift your game. Consider this as a personal branding master class.

This book shares many of the branding strategies that work successfully for large corporations and entities in establishing or promoting their particular brand. But in these pages you are the brand.

In thirty seconds your potential client has judged you and decided whether they like you, whether they trust you and whether they will do business with you. Thirty seconds is a very short time, but within that time you can manage the impressions your clients, audience or colleagues make of you and your business.

Image is defined as how you are perceived by the public. Branding and brand awareness exists in the hearts and minds of your customers, employees and suppliers when they consider your business. That is also how you are perceived by the public. Therefore, throughout this book we use the terms 'image' and 'brand' interchangeably. It is all a matter of how you are perceived.

These branding principles can be applied cross-contextually to a corporation, business owner, professional or executive.

Branding is often perceived as spending a lot of money on logos and advertisements. This book reveals that personal branding does not need to be expensive. Branding is substantially more about the things you do than the things you buy. This is a very important distinction.

You are a product. You are a package ...

Your employer, colleagues, prospects or customers are the consumers of your product. Your job is to influence the consumers of your product to purchase you instead of your competitor. You must tell your target market why they need to choose you over your competitor. Position yourself so there is no alternative. You are the 'only choice' brand.

Personal success relies largely on your ability to communicate ... you can express your potential quietly and effectively without saying a word.

Having your personal brand consistent with your business brand, mission and service standards is essential.
Without a doubt limited resources can be a major issue. Fortunately, changing your personal brand can be inexpensive. You can present an incredibly professional image on a budget.

The best positioning you can have among your prospects and clients is that of an expert; the authority in your area of expertise.

Within this book you will learn how to:

- align your personal brand with client expectations
- build a professional identity that complements your brand
- strengthen your professional effectiveness

This book is especially for you if:

- you are unsure of the appropriate brand to support your goals
- your existing brand does not reflect your potential
- you are having difficulty gaining authority and credibility in your field

Often without the resources of large businesses, small businesses need to think carefully about what image they are presenting to their clients. Likewise with busy professionals and executives, it has become increasingly important to brand yourself separately to the organization you work with as tenure decreases and mobility increases. Branding yourself a key player in your chosen industry becomes paramount for small business, big business, executives and professionals alike.

It is critical to recognize the importance of your personal, professional and business image in building a successful personal brand.

A client's impression of you will determine if they will do business with you.

I believe in both miracles and destiny, but in the end we make our own realities. Branding doesn't happen by deciding it's a good idea. There's a lot of work to do in the pages that follow, and it's a process that will take time. So ... why should you bother? Here's why: To know who you are and be valued for it, to attract what you want, to become more attractive to others, to inspire confidence, to walk your path with integrity, and to distinguish yourself in your chosen field.

Personal branding is a journey in finding your authentic self and your life-purpose. Get ready for a life full of purpose... passion... prosperity.

Chapter 1

What is Personal Branding?

It's not nearly as painful as it sounds. Personal branding has become the latest business tool to accelerate your career success. No longer the turf of celebrities and media personalities, personal branding is the new strategy in leveraging your professional profile and branding yourself as an authority in your chosen field.

Personal branding is simply how we market ourselves. If we were a product, how would we market and promote ourselves? At Jump the Q® Inc. we call it the "Art of Self Packaging".

As Personal Branding Strategists, the number of professionals seeking our services to develop a strategic personal brand and signature style has grown rapidly. Particularly as a result of CEO's such as Donald Trump, Richard Branson, Warren Buffet, Bill Gates and others becoming celebrities in their own right due to their powerful personal brands.

Gone are the days when seeking the services of a professional branding organization were strictly the territory of new product launches and media personalities in crisis requiring a quick re-badge.

Corporate A-listers are now taking professional development notes from celebrities such as Victoria Beckham and Paris Hilton. As individuals, they have created enormous brand equity through purposefully positioning themselves and as a result, have developed very valuable personal brands.

A celebrity is influential when they have a definable style. What is your definable style? What's your signature brand style?

Your personal brand should reflect:

- your abilities
- unique attributes, and
- your potential

'Becoming your own unique brand is essential in today's market!'
— *Rachel Quilty*

If you have an excellent personal brand, reputation and references, then you will be hired first, promoted quicker and afforded more authority and respect. Personal branding also affords you more mobility within your industry, and interestingly, your prices and services are questioned less.

Recruiting firms have introduced personal branding initiatives to niche their well branded candidates as the 'preferred' candidate. You too can become the 'only choice' candidate within your marketplace with a memorable and desirable personal brand.

Richard Branson is one of the most recognized personal brands in the world. The purpose of personal branding is to differentiate you. By working to your strengths and specializing, you amplify your credibility and improve your personal persuasiveness by increasing your perceived value.

To build a successful personal brand, it is essential at this stage to have a solid foundational knowledge of exactly:

- what is personal branding
- why personal branding is important, and
- what contributes to a successful personal brand

We will discuss the latter two topics in greater depth in subsequent chapters.

WHAT IS A BRAND?

A brand is the character of a thing or person as perceived by the public. Brand is also defined as 'to impress indelibly'. A brand is a kind or variety of something that is distinguished by one or more distinctive characteristics.

WHAT IS PERSONAL BRANDING?

Personal branding applies traditional branding concepts to the individual.

Wikipedia® advises us that, 'Personal branding is the process whereby people and their careers are marked as brands. The personal branding concept suggests that success comes from self-packaging. Further defined as the creation of an asset that pertains to a particular person or individual; this includes but is not limited to the body, clothing, appearance and knowledge contained within, leading to an indelible impression that is uniquely distinguishable.'

Tom Peters provides that 'Branding means nothing more (and nothing less) than creating a distinct personality ... and telling the world about it.' While Peter Montoya adds, 'Personal branding is the process that takes your skills, personality and unique characteristics and packages them into a powerful identity that lifts you above the crowd of anonymous competitors.'

Dan Schawbel's book, Web 2.0, provides a more extensive definition of what is personal branding. His collaborators define, personal branding as 'the process by which individuals and entrepreneurs differentiate themselves and stand out from a crowd by identifying and articulating their unique value proposition, whether professional or personal, then leverage it across platforms with a consistent message and image to achieve a specific goal. In this way, individuals can enhance their recognition as experts in their field, establish a reputation and credibility, advance their careers and build self confidence.'

WHAT DOES ALL THAT MEAN TO YOU?

Personal branding is really about how we market ourselves to others. Personal branding is about promoting what is true and unique about you and letting everyone know about it. As a brand, you are your own free agent – you have the freedom to create the career or business path that links your talents and interests with the right purpose and position.

> 'Personal branding is about promoting what is true and unique about you and letting your target audience know about it.'

As an individual, you must acknowledge that you are a brand. And who better to market your personal brand than you? This means that at the end of the day, the success of your personal brand lies in your hands.

A compelling personal brand is one which:

- has an easy identifiable personal identity
- it stimulates a positive emotional response
- it embodies specific desired values or qualities

The goal in designing our personal brand is to discover the strongest and most appealing aspect of our character and then promoting that part of us until we become an embodiment of that trait.

We saw the successful transition of this with Oprah Winfrey's television program. Although rating well during an era of sensational, provocative and obscure topics, Oprah decided to launch a new brand of show. For the past decade, the Oprah show has educated the world on personal responsibility and encouraged personal growth.

Oprah is now the Queen of Personal Responsibility. She has regularly apologized to audiences, taken personal responsibility for book selections and incidents within her organizations, as well as admitted some very personal information in an effort to maintain her integrity with her audience.

- This has allowed Oprah to personify her personal brand and remain true to her values. She truly embodies the principle of taking personal responsibility for your choices.

Our personal brand should never be expressed in terms of our profession, trade or craft. This is because our personal brand far transcends what we do for a living. Our profession just happens to be the forum in which our personal brand is expressed.

Let's briefly go through some branding fundamentals.

The two major elements for measuring and building your brand are:

1. <u>Your Personal Brand Identity</u>: brand name, brand associations, messages, image, environment, symbolism
2. <u>Your Personal Brand Name Awareness:</u> exists in the minds and hearts of your customers, employees, and suppliers

A good personal brand:

- gives a good first impression
- is easy to remember
- evokes positive associations

The purpose of a brand is to:

- differentiate yourself, and
- achieve your desired results

Your personal brand is the result of a combination of impressions held about your name, expertise and professional image.

These impressions are derived from factors including:

- physical appearance such as logo, colors, office, attire and vehicles
- your attitudes, beliefs and values and how these are reflected in your performance, actions and activities, and
- how you express yourself to your clients, market and community

For success you must manage your total brand. This broadly comprises your performance, presentation, attitude, communication skills and reputation. These are the vital areas of your 'brand' from which we are all judged.

You cannot always control your brand completely because your personal brand is based on the perceptions of others such as clients or potential clients, but you <u>can</u> control your personal brand identity.

Brand identity is basically the look, feel and performance of the brand. These are within your control. However, how people perceive them is not always in your control.

It is often said, 'If you look good, your product will be good, your prices will be good and your client service will be good.'

With skilful planning, your personal brand identity allows you to tell your audience what you want to say about yourself and how you want to be perceived. A good personal brand identity will visually separate and distinguish you and your products and services from all others. In a sense, your brand is your destiny, and by controlling your brand you have taken a big step in controlling your destiny.

'In a sense your brand is your destiny, and by controlling your brand you have taken a big step in controlling your destiny.'

THE POWER OF A PERSONAL BRAND

Personal branding is simply positioning and marketing you favorably. Steve Van Yoder of 'Get Slightly Famous' fame outlines that brands have a number of strategic functions, thus enabling you to:

- differentiate yourself from your competitors
- position your message in the hearts and minds of your target customers
- persist and be consistent in your marketing efforts
- customize your services to reflect your personal brand
- deliver your message clearly and quickly
- project credibility
- strike an emotional chord
- create strong user loyalty

Jump the Q®'s **Brand Yourself Action Plan**, identifies ten vital Action Steps to design, create and build a powerful and persuasive brand. The process we outline leads you through these Action Steps to position, build and market your best personal brand.

We recommend that you commit to completing the following **Brand Yourself Action Plan** so that you can dominate your marketplace. The Action Steps are:

Action Step 1.   Discover your existing personal brand
Action Step 2.   Determine your brand's target audience
Action Step 3.   Define your true personal brand
Action Step 4.   Dominate your market as the authority
Action Step 5.   Design your unique personal brand
Action Step 6.   Develop your brand's signature style
Action Step 7.   Devise your personal brand marketing plan
Action Step 8.   Decide your desired outcomes, resources and skill set
Action Step 9.   Deploy your personal brand message
Action Step 10. Deliver your personal brand promise

Each step will be discussed in greater detail in the later chapters.

POSITION YOURSELF WITH YOUR PERSONAL BRAND

You should develop the habit of continually thinking about how you are positioned in the hearts and minds of your client. Your brand should identify you as a leader and therefore, should be distinctive and visible as well as being consistent.

Within the **Brand Yourself Action Plan**, we consider the principles of positioning your personal brand as an **AUTHORITY** in your industry or field.

Briefly the principles are:

A = Attributes
U = Unique
T = Territory
H = Hook
O = Opportunity
R = Reliability
I = Image
T = Trustworthy
Y = Yourself

Personal branding differs from image management as it relies on consciously creating an image to fit with others' expectations. Personal branding is founded in a sincere and authentic communication of who you are. It is important that you ensure your image and brand accurately reflects you, your potential and your desired results.

Strategic image management is the deliberate and favorable impression created to assist others to believe the evidence of what they see. If you present yourself visually and behaviorally as a successful person, others will respond to you accordingly.

The first step to building a successful personal brand is to determine what your current image really is. We all have an image and the challenge is to develop an accurate picture of you as perceived by others.

Within Action Step 1 we investigate your current brand and brand equity. Your reputation or 'brand equity' is one of the few resources that you have with a sustainable competitive advantage.

Your reputation is an asset to be created, nurtured and used to your advantage.

This increased perceived value allows you to 'premium price' your services. Research has also indicated that seventy percent of a market is willing to pay an additional twenty percent premium on branded products, and forty percent have indicated a willingness to pay a thirty percent premium.

Improving your professional image and personal brand is an investment in building your personal profile, reputation and the results you will achieve. And deserve to achieve.

'Improving your professional image and personal brand is an investment in building your personal profile, reputation and the results you will achieve. And deserve to achieve.' — *Rachel Quilty*

Chapter 2

Why is Personal Branding so Important?

Personal branding is the most powerful success and business building tool ever devised. Within this chapter we consider why personal branding is important and what elements create an effective personal brand.

Within the next chapter we look at some of the attributes that are commonly evidenced in great personal brands.

WHY IS BRAND IMAGE SO IMPORTANT?

Why does someone's perception of our personal brand matter? In less than a minute, we have made an indelible impression. In those first few seconds of connecting, a person makes up their mind about us.

They decide whether they:

- like us
- trust us
- want to spend time us, and
- want to do business with us

In fact, research indicates that sixty-seven percent of first impressions are accurate. Is your first impression an accurate reflection of your personal brand?

A person's first impression is more important than a combination of their next five or six encounters with us. This highlights the importance of accurate first impressions and having a clear under-standing of how the psychology of a first impression works. We will discuss this further when we detail the Halo and Horn Effect.

The message is simple. We are the product – and our fate may be sealed before we've even said a word. We are "seen" and "judged" in an instant. From our image, people determine our apparent level of:

- ability
- success
- credibility
- sophistication
- self-confidence
- self-esteem
- education
- seniority
- social and moral values
- social standing
- charisma
- authority

You may say, "People should not judge me by the way I look on the outside. It's about my abilities and attitude." This is a nice idea, but the fact is that you also judge everyone you meet by the way they look, too. The first impression is believed even if it's not true.
Why? Because we all like to be ... right! And we like the comfort that being right brings into our lives. After all, we are in control.

We often hear that it doesn't matter what other people think.

Are you too vain to care? Apparently, it's not your business what others think about you. Maybe that's true. But your reputation is your most precious commodity.

You must be concerned about the way you look and appear to others. You must be concerned about what people say and think about you. You should be concerned about earning and keeping the esteem and respect of the important people in your life.

It has been said that everything you do is carried out to earn the respect of people who you respect, or at least to not lose their respect.

Everyone judges by the visual images presented to them. Personal success relies largely on our ability to communicate ... you can express your potential quietly and effectively without saying a word.

Your personal brand is a reflection of what you're capable of.

> Your personal brand is a reflection of what you're capable of.
> — *Rachel Quilty*

Why build a personal brand? Why is branding yourself the best solution? Why is personal branding so important?

The answer to these questions is that personal branding allows you to take control of your identity, and influence the impression that people have of you. This helps you accomplish any number of the following:

- build a powerful personal brand
- create a brand that attracts clients
- develop a personal brand that reflects your potential and goals
- premium price yourself through differentiation
- brand yourself an industry-thought leader
- accelerate your career success
- position you as the authority in your marketplace
- dominate your niche, and
- become a celebrity in your own field

Through your personal brand, you also have the opportunity to stand out, make a name for yourself and make a difference in your community. Developing your personal brand makes you a more valuable asset, whether within your organization or your own business.

If you build a strong memorable brand, opportunities for success will follow. Personal branding allows you to focus your life's goals to create a powerful package called "insert your name here".

When you strategically manage expectations of your personal brand through your deliberate attributes, actions and non-actions, you become a compelling and captivating personal brand. The goal is for you to be known entirely for who you are as a person and what you stand for.

Personal branding is about creating an identity that influences how prospects, customers, and decision makers perceive you. Personal branding instantly reveals who you are, what you do, and creates perceived value. In a world overwhelmed by messages, a personal brand makes you impossible to ignore.

Personal branding can:

- tell your prospects why they should choose you over someone else
- control how other people perceive you
- influence what others think of you
- tell prospects what you stand for

Once you have created a powerful, compelling personal brand, business comes to you instead of having to rely on your ability to track down prospects and clients. A personal brand can act as a "proxy" of you. It represents you in the minds of prospects and decision makers. It creates perceptions of positive value in the minds of your target market and gives them reasons to choose you.

YOUR FIRST IMPRESSION

First impressions count. Within six seconds a person has formed an opinion. We have made an irreversible first impression.

A first impression is made up of:

- fifty-five percent visual
- thirty-eight percent tonality
- seven percent the words we use

In reality, it's less about what we say, but rather how we actually say it.

Every one of us has a preferred learning or representational system. We are primarily visual, auditory, kinesthetic or audio digital. Approximately sixty percent of people are visual. That means, sixty percent of people who we contact will take in our appearance. They usually are the people who can tell you what everyone was wearing at a networking function.

Keep in mind most people will firstly judge you by what you wear, then how you speak, then the words you say. Every day people judge you – before you have said a word. Before you have said a word your appearance has said a lot about you. The question is, what is it saying about you?

THE HALO EFFECT

It is important to understand that all individuals draw conclusions, an immediate emotional decision is made and then we justify it logically. For example:

- our minds are like pigeon holes, labels and stereotypes
- we like to understand things
- we are very quick to notice things which are not right, seem out of place or different. What's not appropriate!

If you have a positive personal brand, you are attributed with other positive aspects. This is known as the Halo Effect.

For example, if you look confident, you will be perceived as competent and intelligent. You are likely to be a nice person. Good at your job. You will be good to do business with. People will be more willing to accept your prices and will question you less.

The Halo Effect also is seen in a greater willingness by others to forgive transgressions.

A more significant aspect of the psychology of a first impression is that within later encounters we track and recognize actions or behavior that supports our first impression, validating our first decision. Even if it was wrong.

If we create a negative first impression, it takes a lot of work to change it. If you don't have a positive image people, will challenge your product, prices and question your service and quality. You will not be afforded the same opportunities, promotions and attention. This is called the Horn Effect.

> An OPSM® television advertisement provides an excellent illustration of the power of branding. The sales assistant initially seems young and incapable of helping a more mature customer. The customer perceiving a lack of expertise and authority requests her supervisor. The same sales assistant returns from the back office with her hair up and glasses looking more professional and credible. She is immediately afforded more respect by the customer.

Isn't that amazing ... same person, different personal brand, different image, different manner, and the outcome is a different perception of abilities. This happens every day.

Your personal brand directly influences:

- your thinking
- what you feel
- your behavior, and
- others you interact with and their thoughts, feelings and behavior

Therefore, your personal brand directly affects your reputation and others' perception of you.

Often our personal brand identity and what our brand stands for are more influential than our track record. We often say in the industry, "An ounce of image is worth a ton of performance." Never believe that your output is of more value than your personal branding and professional image.

A great track record of performance built on intelligence, skill and hard work is certainly a prerequisite for delivering your brand promise. However, a positive, professional personal brand that ignites people, mobilizes them into action and influences public opinion is what's even more important.

IMPRESSIONS TRANSLATE INTO ACTION

If you have an excellent brand, reputation and references, you will be:

- hired or engaged first
- promoted quicker
- afforded more authority and respect
- your suggestions will be given more weight
- your word becomes your bond
- you will be respected

Interestingly enough, you do not have to be in a senior position and ranking – highly respected people in any position are given greater authority.

The right personal brand can:

- help you achieve your business goals
- improve your business credibility and positioning
- improve your communication and persuasiveness
- increase your confidence and effectiveness
- earn you improved market standing and success

You can save money by improving all aspects of your personal brand. Improving your professional image has a direct effect of improving your perceived professionalism and the quality of your brand.

Individuals, who have a professional image, are appropriately attired and/or have the trappings of authority, are accorded more attention or obedience by those they encounter ... a fact confirmed by many studies. Improving your professional image and in turn your personal brand increases your persuasiveness.

It is likely you are not taking advantage of this principle. Consequently, you are undervaluing and, very possibly, underselling yourself and/or your business and your personal brand.

YOUR BRAND TRANSLATES INTO DOLLARS

A study was conducted where identical resumes were sent to recruiters accompanied by different photos. The study revealed the professional image had an important impact on the salaries received and offered. The applicants with the more professional and groomed image were offered from eight to twenty percent greater salaries then those perceived as less professional due to their grooming and professional image.

Are you sabotaging your earning potential?

BUILD YOUR PERSONAL BRAND EQUITY

When you communicate with purpose you begin to build your brand edge. As we mentioned earlier, seventy percent of the market is prepared to pay a twenty percent premium on branded products, and forty percent would pay a thirty percent premium. The preparedness of clients to pay a premium to engage you is considered your personal brand equity.

> The preparedness of clients to pay a premium to engage you is considered your personal brand equity.
> — *Rachel Quilty*

The basic definition of personal brand equity is the level of positive, residual emotional feeling others have about us and our personal brand. If others have strong, positive feelings about you, then you have accumulated a significant amount of personal brand equity.

The converse is also true. We build personal brand equity by practising consistent behavior over time that reinforces the message we want others to think when they think of us.

Your brand equity is simply the difference in premium you are able to charge due to your branding when compared to a generic brand or the average cost charged within your field. By building your personal brand, over time you are able to premium price your services. In recruiting circles, this premium paid is called "love money".

You can see how quickly your brand equity can increase and just how easy it is to build. Don't forget your reputation is your brand equity. It is your promise to clients and a guarantee of your value.

In essence, you can control your bottom line ... because you control the message! Take control of your personal brand and start naming your price. When your reputation precedes you and you become the "only choice" brand you establish a significant competitive advantage.

CREATE A COMPETITIVE ADVANTAGE

Developing a strong personal brand provides a lasting competitive advantage. A great personal brand is more focused and creates a powerful reserve of good will for the times when we make an error. Personal branding is an extremely effective tool because it centralizes all of our business development, career advancement and marketing efforts. Powerful results can be achieved from proper focus and consistent and persistent effort.

This competitive advantage allows our brand to gain the "edge" over its competition.

BUILDING YOUR PERSONAL BRAND EDGE

Brand advantage comes when your target market believes that the brand:

- listens to them and cares for them
- reliably delivers what it promises
- is always interesting by being different or innovative
- wraps up any deals smoothly and simply
- is happy and projects this happiness

People want to see your human side before they will accept your brand fully. They want to see emotion, enthusiasm, passion or personality in your communication.

More than seventy percent of us do not care for advertising. We are looking instead for the human touch. Too many marketers have forgotten one simple truth – human communication is one of our greatest needs.

To build our brand edge, we must design a strategic message and deliver a well considered communication plan to establish an effective, results orientated personal brand.

WHAT MAKES AN EFFECTIVE PERSONAL BRAND?

An effective overall personal brand is one that is:

- credible
- congruent
- attractive
- appropriate
- confident
- consistent
- of a positive stereotype

Let's look at each of these terms in more detail and how they apply to our personal brand.

Credible

What does your audience want to see? What kind of packaging does it respond to, feel safe with, understand, respect and admire? What kind of package can you put together to motivate or influence your audience?

Conduct your own market research to find out what your target audience finds attractive, reassuring, non-threatening, "professional", or cool. Now, this will be different for different markets.

You are going to need to package yourself in a way that is complementary to your industry's standard to maintain credibility. But you should look current and stylish to the degree that's acceptable in your field and in your environment.

Congruent

Ensure that your professional image, performance, attitude and behaviors are branding your business and reflecting your products and/or services' market position. Your overall total public image should be consistent with your brand.

A good business identity will visually separate and distinguish a company and its products and services from all others. In a sense identity is destiny, and by controlling your identity, you have taken a big step in controlling your destiny.

Strive to meet the expectations and sophistication level of the top person within the group you are going to interact with. You cannot always completely control your brand because image is based on the perceptions of others such as clients or potential clients, but you can control your brand identity.

Brand identity is basically the look, feel and performance of the brand. These are within your control. However, how people perceive them is not always in your control.

Attractive
It has been proven that more confident, professional and well groomed people are more persuasive. Like attracts like! Build rapport. Use the "just like me" factor.

They say, "If you look good, your product will be good, your prices will be good and your client service will be good." When planned, your brand identity allows you to tell your audience what you want to say about yourself and how you want to be perceived.

Your total public image should be consistent with your message. Presenting a professional image is a direct reflection on you.

- Do you care about yourself?
- Are you disciplined?
- Do you provide attention to detail?
- How will you treat a client?

Appropriateness

When designing your brand, your challenge is twofold: to make your exterior appealing to your target audience and to make sure your exterior is as much a genuine reflection of your interior as possible.

Designing an appropriately appealing personal brand for your target audience signals that you are aware of your client's expectations and understand their needs, wants and desires. Your personal brand must deliver a message that communicates your position, your understanding of the industry and business occasion as well as the message that you wish to transmit about your brand.

Confident

When you look good, appear comfortable with yourself and are congruent with your personal brand statement, your packaging can then recede from attention and others can focus on you and the conversation. This focuses clients on the relevancy of your products and services rather than on the question of whether they want to do business with you as they consider your overall presentation.

So be competent, be prepared and be confident in your abilities. Knowledge is the surest way to make a credible name for yourself as you become the recognized expert. You can leverage that knowledge into a halo of authority. These can cement your place as the leader in your market niche. Always ensure you are neat and well groomed and do not provide distractions from your message.

Self-confidence and the appearance of self-confidence is a brand's more powerful strategy. The confident mindset is an incredible propeller in all aspects of life.

Confidence is a self fulfilling prophecy. Confidence is sexy and wildly attractive.

Just look at the impact of Paris Hilton's confidence on her personal brand equity. Customers flock to a confident brand. It is also very important to maintain people's confidence in your brand by being congruent and trustworthy.

Jim Rohn accurately highlights, *"Effective communication is twenty percent what you know and eighty percent how you feel about what you know."*

> Effective communication is twenty percent what you know and eighty percent how you feel about what you know.
>
> — *Jim Rohn*

Consistent

Creating a consistent brand is important. Your personal brand is a reflection of what you're capable of. Is your brand an accurate and consistent reflection of your abilities and potential? Your message and your performance must be consistent.

Research has shown time and again there is a direct correlation between a product's level of awareness and its market share. Even more fascinating is the fairly common perception that a better known product is a better product ... whether it is or not.

> Research has shown time and again, there is a direct correlation between a product's level of awareness and its market share.
>
> — *Rachel Quilty*

In order to create perceptions, a consistent flow of information is needed to raise awareness. Remember, your goal is to control the flow of information about you, and to do that you must provide information that clearly defines your business, which in turn is you!

Keeping up a steady flow of information increases your chances of influencing what people think about you, your product, service or company. The absence of such information leaves it for your critics and competitors to define your business.

Brand consistency is critical to developing brand loyalty. Brand inconsistency erodes confidence. So you must develop habits and activities that support your personal brand tone. And it's essential that your personal brand is consistent with your business brand, mission and service standards.

Positive Stereotype

Stereotypes can make a lasting impression. If you look like you belong to a certain group you will be perceived as having the same attitudes and characteristics associated with that group's public image. So choose your stereotype carefully.

Ask yourself, "What are the characteristics associated with the brand I want to project?"

Remember that social psychologists say first impressions are made up of fifty-five percent visual input. Visual impressions are important and are an integral part of the communication process. Visual aspects of your business such as vehicles, staff attire, workspaces and stationery should reflect your overall elected business image and your personal brand.

Selecting the right design and identity for your personal brand has a huge impact on your personal or business success. In the next chapter, we investigate how adopting the right attitude and developing attributes that are characteristic of great personal brands can help your personal brand thrive.

Chapter 3

What Makes a Successful Personal Brand?

Your financial success and celebrity status with your target audience are greatly influenced by how compelling your personal brand is. Success is the subtext for this book. Success means different things for different people. However, it is always a process of self-actualization.

The process of branding allows you to become the person you were meant to be. Branding makes you an active partner in fulfilling your destiny in business and in life.

Most would agree that success does not result from intelligence nor results alone. We've all seen brilliant people fade into mediocrity. Nor does it arise solely from great clothes, effective people skills or a good attitude.

True and lasting success depends on the totality of your personal brand. Your total brand is made up of these five essential elements which must be managed for long term success of your personal brand. They are:

1. your hidden image – your attitude, ability, self esteem
2. your assumed image – your reputation
3. your visual image – your packaging and appearance
4. your experienced image – your communication skills
5. your proven image – you over a period of time

The total "experience" a client has with you, your personal brand and your products or services will determine your success. The buying decisions of clients are based on value and image. However, attaining and maintaining a good image can't be an end in itself.

The first rule of effective personal branding is not just to look good, but also to be good. Every organization, regardless of size is challenged to remain differentiated, significant and relevant.

WINNING QUALITIES OF A SUCCESSFUL BRAND?

Effective people self-market for career reasons to increase name recognition, build a reputation, help promote their employer, get new clients and gain a prestigious social standing, allowing them to further their beliefs.

Establishing a well known name and a public reputation allows you to take advantage of our culture's obsession with fame and celebrity.

You need to approach your brand in terms of differentiation. In other words, standing out from the crowd and marketability – that is, providing other people what they want or need. Why should someone choose your brand?

As tangible differences in actual services and products diminish, the client perception of an organization and their product or services has now become the key market place differentiator. Increasingly, your branding and brand awareness become essential to your personal success.

The successful personal brand has the right mix of confidence, passion, likeability, determination, and focus. When you look at successful business leaders, you realize that each has a self-purpose, a call to action and a desire to win.

Within this chapter, we will look at thirteen qualities consistently found in the most successful people on the planet. These qualities are:

1. being committed
2. being passionate
3. being courageous
4. being comfortable with being uncomfortable
5. keeping your eye on the big picture
6. keeping the right company
7. keeping a conscious leader mindset
8. keeping your faith
9. maintaining a great attitude
10. maintaining a prophetic stance
11. maintaining a disciplined approach
12. maintaining a continuous improvement program
13. maintaining a healthy attitude about change

Model yourself on these attributes. After all Jim Rohn has said, *"Success is not to be pursued; it is to be attracted by the person you become."*

BEING COMMITTED

Branding yourself requires and demands total commitment. You've got to be willing to step outside of your business or career and focus on brand building, instead of selling and advertising. You must dedicate a certain number of hours each week to activities which will grow your personal brand.

Sir Richard Branson, CEO of the Virgin Group, the most personable personal branding in the world notes the following, *"Branding demands commitment; commitment to continual re-invention; striking chords with people to stir their emotions; and commitment to imagination. It is easy to be cynical about such things, much harder to be successful."*

You need to become your own brand strategist. Personal branding takes time - up to twelve months to design and create your brand, develop your brand tools, and get your message out to your target market. If you remain focused on the long term goal and are purposeful in your weekly activities, your personal brand will change your life forever.

The essential ingredient to your commitment to your brand is to be well prepared. This is extremely important as it can assist you overcome your fears. Fear arises from a previous negative experience or a lack of preparation; that is, fear of the unknown, or ignorance in a loving sense, that what you haven't already experienced will create a level of anxiety.

It will keep you in good stead to become obsessed with your goals and your brand. Your brand becomes your own magnificent obsession. Some of the most successful brands and individuals become household names through their complete focus on a task. Thomas Edison famously claimed to have discovered nearly a thousand ways not to create a light bulb. Henry Ford became focused on delivering an affordable car to every American family. Microsoft planned to have a computer in every household.

You'll see a familiar trend within the following quotes:

"I know quite certainly that I myself have no special talent; curiosity, obsession and dogged endurance, combined with self-criticism, have brought me to my ideas." — Albert Einstein

"I'm a guy who just wanted to see his name in the line up every day. To me, baseball was a passion to the point of obsession." — Brooks Robinson

"I've been called many names like perfectionist, difficult and obsessive. I think it takes obsession, takes searching for the details for any artist to be good." — Barbra Streisand

"What moves those of genius, what inspires their work is not new ideas, but their obsession with the idea that what has already been said is still not enough." — Eugene Delacroix

"Your ability to use the principle of autosuggestion will depend, very largely, upon your capacity to concentrate upon a given desire until that desire becomes a burning obsession." — Napoleon Hill

The action in commitment is in the doing. That is where the magic is! When we consider great or iconic personal brands they stood for something – a quality that touched their audience's hearts.

If you want to be a mini celebrity in your field, you must establish a commitment about building your personal brand equity that borders on obsession.

BEING PASSIONATE

Passion is very appealing and compelling. We are drawn almost magnetically to people who are passionate, people who are in love with what they do.

Passion may mean many things – zeal, enthusiasm, excitement – or it may be a gentler message which is persistence, obsession.

> Enthusiasm is contagious. Be the person that everyone wants to spend time with.
> — *Rachel Quilty*

The words of Henry Ford should ring true in your life, *"I do not believe a man can ever leave his business. He ought to think of it by day and dream of it by night."*

For those of you who feel that obsession errs on the extreme side of life, this quote is for you. I urge you to become passionate about your brand. Paul Carvel once said, *"Passion is a positive obsession. Obsession is a negative passion"*.

Passion can drive change and can change a reality. Use your passion to make a change in your life and your community.

BEING COURAGEOUS

Fear stops us in our tracks. Often the one thing you are afraid of is the one thing you need to do to solidify your brand. The biggest fears on earth are:

- fear of rejection
- fear of success, and
- fear of failure

Develop a list of internal and external fears or limitations to the success of your brand.

Courage is defined as taking action despite the fear. Recognize areas of anxiety and move forward regardless.

I love this quote attributed to Angelina Jolie, *"If you ask people what they've always wanted to do, most people haven't done it. That breaks my heart."*

Sometimes despite your fears, you have to commit and concede to a greater authority and just know that it is the right thing to do.

The more you think about what you are doing, the more familiar it all becomes. The more familiar you become ... the less fearful you will be. Talk about your dream with family and friends. You may want to:

- talk about it
- work on it
- plan and write about it
- visualize it, and
- capture your dream on a vision board

Then go and live your dream!

> One of the greatest discoveries a man makes, one of his great surprises, is to find he can do what he was afraid he couldn't do.
> — *Henry Ford*

BEING COMFORTABLE WITH BEING UNCOMFORTABLE

Every successful person has had to take a deep breath and step into the spotlight. Many of the most confident and accomplished people in the world will admit to nerves. Yet when we consider their performance, we wouldn't know it.

When you look good and appear comfortable with yourself, your appearance can then recede from attention and others can focus on you and the conversation.

Keep a victory file with confidence building reference points for yourself.

Save articles, reviews, certificates of merit, thank you letters, letter of recommendation or appreciation or congratulations ... and keep them in a victory file. Any time you feel your faith being tested, pull out your victory file and review it ... this will reinstall your confidence.

Paris Hilton in her book, *Confessions of an Heiress* says *"Being an heiress is really all in your head. If you follow your own plans and dreams and you don't let anyone talk you out of them, then you'll start to get the hang of being an heiress. It's all about feeling entitled, which seems ... to make a big impression – a good one.*

"Heiresses are born with privileges. Channel your own inner heiress, create your own image, and project extreme sense of confidence - even if you don't really feel it every moment - people will treat you differently. Put yourself on your own pedestal and then everybody else will, too."

Always act like you're on camera, and the spotlights are on you. Always behave like you are the centre of attention. As Brian Tracy says, *"If you look like a winner, you act and feel like a winner."*

> The few who do are the envy of the many who only watch.
> — *Jim Rohn*

KEEPING YOUR EYE ON THE BIG PICTURE.

Successful people with strong brands keep their eye on the big picture and don't get seduced by the details and distractions that will be presented along the way. Another way of looking at this is to determine what your assignment here on earth is and prioritize your focus on activities that support that. This is a key to change.

Anything that takes us off task may be an issue to be addressed. An emotional pull or constant distraction away from our purpose is likely the very thing we need to conquer in our lives. We all have a life-purpose to fulfill and it's big! Our personal growth journey is to continually conquer the issues that arise on our mission to complete that purpose.

Donald Trump has said, *"Tough times should never prevent you from thinking big. To make it simple: if you are going to be thinking anyway, you may as well think big. Most people think small because most people are afraid of success, afraid of making decisions and afraid of winning. And that gives people like me a great advantage."*

The super successful people in this world have had big dreams. They were conscious of the skills, contacts, and the hard work that would be needed to achieve that dream and created a plan. And then they worked their plan.

You don't live your dream; you work toward your dream.

KEEPING THE RIGHT COMPANY

Anyone whose success depends upon the cooperation of another person must have a great personal brand if they hope to be successful. Know who your friends are and avoid those people who may undermine your credibility or brand. Remember gossips gossip about the people they were most recently with. If people gossip to you, they will gossip about you. Avoid these types. Distinguish them from positive, talkative types who are likely to let twenty people know how wonderful you are.

Remember who you spend time with is also a reflection of your brand. Are they the type of person who represents your brand and is a positive connection?

In creating a successful brand you must actively recruit supporters. Surround yourself with people who support your dream, are committed to your success and who are willing to aid your brand goals.

Behind every great leader was a great mentor. The bigger our personal brand grows, the more important it is to have reliable confidants who are not afraid to tell us when we have stepped out of line.

Connecting and actively taking and implementing the advice of your mentors can really put you in the big league. An endorsement from them could really kick start your new level of success.

KEEPING A CONSCIOUS LEADERSHIP MINDSET

Decide to become the CEO of your life and position yourself as the authority in your field and decide what legacy you want to achieve. A conscious leadership mindset starts with taking personal responsibility for your thoughts, actions and results. After all, how can we lead others if we can't lead ourselves?

I love the quote from Brian Klemmer's book, *The Compassionate Samurai*, in which he says *"the only problem you have, is the one you haven't fixed yet"*. That is personal responsibility in action. That is a true leader.

Remember the first rule of self-image psychology. "The person you see is the person you will be." Your self-image, that is, the person you see yourself as on the inside, will determine how you behave on the outside. As Brian Tracy outlines, a major part of your self-concept is your self-image.

This is made up of three elements:

1. the way you see yourself
2. the way that others see you, and
3. the way that you would like to be seen by others

The self-image is the key to human personality and human behavior. Change the self-image and you change the personality and the behavior.

We can develop a conscious leadership mindset for our personal brand by deciding to become the authority in our marketplace and work consistently towards that goal. Zig Ziglar, correctly determined that, *"When your [self] image improves, your performance improves"*.

The principles of positioning will create you as a powerful, positive and persuasive brand and the authority in your industry or field. We will look more closely at the principles of positioning your personal brand in a later chapter.

> "When your image improves, your performance improves."
> *— Zig Ziglar*

KEEPING YOUR FAITH

When you think of the greatest brands in the world – Jesus Christ, Gandhi, Nelson Mandela, Mother Theresa, Oprah and the list goes on – consider the spiritual backbone that supported these people through some of the most horrific experiences. Their faith in their true purpose sustained them through great hardship.

Often they found peace in dire situations by trusting that inner spirit and voice that all would be well. They accepted that they did not have all the answers in circumstances that were out of their control. In fact, they were provided strength and a guiding light by trusting in a power greater than themselves.

We are all made of body, mind and soul. We are often quick to recognize and support our body and mind. Yet we neglect our soul or our spiritual health.

Are you neglecting your spiritual health?

As an avid reader of personal autobiographies and biographies, I am continually reminded that faith and belief in a higher power is an essential ingredient to personal success and to attaining the most incredible achievements.

MAINTAINING A GREAT ATTITUDE

A killer attitude has launched many famous brands.
Take an attitude assessment. What attitude do you take into the day with you?

Having a good attitude often means being comfortable with being uncomfortable. Attitude is also about having an opinion and taking a stand. Determine what you are and what you are not!

Decide what attitude traits do not reflect your brand and what traits you do want to develop so that your brand can progress in a more positive direction.

Radiate interest, energy, enthusiasm, good humor and good will. Sometimes we may not feel inclined, but we know when we've made the extra effort in the past we have enjoyed it. Arriving with the right attitude can change everything. You attract that attitude back, so be conscious of which attitude you choose to adopt.

Being charismatic! We are all born with the ability to be charismatic – it's just whether we are prepared to develop it. Those who are said to have charisma have also consciously worked to generate and develop it.

It's easy to build personal brand equity when we are in a great mood. But the real measure of character is finding ways to get it done when nothing seems to be going right. When the odds are stacked against us, we need coping tools to sustain a positive attitude.

The more successful we become, the more grateful we need to be. When people show us their support, admiration and trust – do not take them for granted. Never miss an opportunity to display your gratitude even when you don't feel like it.

A great personal brand embodies honour and inspires others to action. True honour involves humility, self-awareness and discipline to do the right thing.

MAINTAINING A PROPHETIC STANCE

The leaders with the most influential personal brands have always decided for themselves what they want their personal brand to be. They are also very intentional and passionate about promoting their personal brand with their target audience.

What are you regularly thinking or stating about your life? Pay attention to your thoughts and your idle comments. Become focused and conscious of your thoughts and feelings. Take control of them.

Some interesting comments made famous through their fulfilment. Madonna, was asked, "What next?" after her number one album, *Like a Virgin* was released. Madonna replied, *"I want to rule the world"*. Oprah is often quoted as saying, *"I want to be loved by everyone"*. Marilyn Monroe, loved by the world, once said, *"I am not interested in money. I just want to be wonderful"*.
And Warren Buffett, in one interview when questioned about his amazing wealth said, *"I always knew I was going to be rich. I don't think I ever doubted it for a minute"*.

What are you prophesying over your life?

MAINTAINING A DISCIPLINED APPROACH

Become the CEO of your life. If you don't, who will? We must all suffer one of two things: the pain of discipline or the pain of regret or disappointment.

Woody Allen and Donald Trump have both observed that a large percentage of success is just showing up. Maintaining and building your personal brand is really about having the discipline to keep to your schedule, your commitments and your promises. The greatest freedom is achieved through discipline. You can create a quality life by fulfilling your promises and honouring your word.

Take heart from the following quotes:

"Effective leadership is putting first things first. Effective management is discipline, carrying it out."   — Stephen R. Covey

"Success is nothing more than a few simple disciplines, practiced every day. Discipline is the bridge between goals and accomplishment."
                                                            — Jim Rohn

Natural talent will take you so far. You then have to have the character to discipline yourself to cultivate and improve that talent.

MAINTAINING A CONTINUOUS IMPROVEMENT PROGRAM

Great personal brands go on to become outstanding personal brands through the development of their character. When we consider the great names of history, it is due to their character as opposed to their ability and talent that they remained successful, became great and left enormous legacies. The truly great leaders of this world possessed two things, a sense of urgency and a hunger to learn from others.

Often the people who make the most money are not the most technically competent. But what they lack in technical competency they make up for in personal brand appeal.

The bottom line is that a little bit of success and a great personal brand will usually go a lot farther than a great performance record and minimal personal brand appeal.

Ensure you and your team complete two personal development / educational programs per year so that everyone continues to grow.

Sometimes noticeable change can take a long time. Make it your quest to improve in a number of areas every day. This could simply be listening, or responding quickly. Look to consistently making small improvements every day. Don't equate slow progress to no progress. Be patient.

As Zig Ziglar says, *"Your input determines your output"*. Reading books and listening to audio books is the best strategy for keeping your chin up no matter what the circumstances.

MAINTAINING A HEALTHY ATTITUDE ABOUT CHANGE

The only constant is change. Change builds character. In the future, the old you will not exist. To move into your purpose you will have to change. Perhaps old habits, old thinking patterns or old relationships may have to change.

What does your future life look like? What does the new you look like? What are some of the thoughts, attributes, actions and behaviors this person would have?

To change things you have to change. To become the person you want to be, what changes need to occur? What boundaries or new guidelines need to be put in place?

Change is the only constant. Standing still is not an option. So the only way to ensure you achieve success and the fulfilment of your dreams is to evolve yourself over time.

Consider the challenges you are experiencing. How do they make you feel? And what is the gain you get when these challenges happen? What belief of yours is reinforced when you experience these challenges?

Often at the heart of a challenge is the decision we made that we are not good enough or we don't deserve better or we are not worthy. You are good enough. You are worth it. You deserve it.

Within the next chapter, we look at you the individual and why you are worth it. We answer the most important question: "Why Brand Yourself for Success?"

Chapter 4

Why Brand Yourself for Success?

The very heart of personal branding is to define who you really are. This means that to build a strong brand requires a clear understanding of your true authentic self. Your personal brand is shaped by your core values, passions, personal characteristics or traits, unique and signature talents, accomplishments and your goals. To be authentic is to be transparent. You, therefore, need to represent yourself accurately at all times.

This is the surprising aspect of personal branding that most people don't appreciate until they start the journey. Personal branding is about discovering and designing the very best you. If for no other reason, branding yourself for success is imperative.

While the end results of building a successful personal brand may equate to being able to:

- develop a personal brand that reflects
  your potential and goals
- premium price yourself through differentiation
- brand yourself an industry leader

In essence, your personal brand means:

- being true to yourself
- fulfilling your dreams
- living your dream lifestyle
- following your true purpose
- owning your dream
- narrowing your focus
- discovering your true worth
- prizing your value
- being of service

Let's look at each of these personal brand outcomes in more detail.

BEING TRUE TO YOURSELF

What would you really, truly like to be doing with your life? Forget about your career for a minute. What would you really like to be doing? Dare to have dreams. And then dare to let them come true. Your great passion may not be achievable during work hours, but there is no reason it cannot be achieved out of work hours. Consistency, clarity and authenticity are the keystones to a great brand.

Be yourself. Be authentic. Authenticity begins with a true acceptance of the real you.

> I am the master of my fate. The captain of my soul.
> — *Invictus (WE Henley)*

Life is an evolution. Often, we do not know our life-purpose immediately. More often, walking through the personal branding action steps facilitates the deeper understanding of your life-purpose as we start to focus on defining your personal brand.

Personal branding is not about creating a false image; it's about unearthing and maximizing your true strengths, values and passions in support of your goals.

Personal branding enables you to define and communicate your area of expertise. Personal branding enables you to align what you do and how you do it with your individuality.

FULFILLING YOUR DREAMS

Your personal success may be reflected in your financial success. Or it may not! As we tell every client, our definitions of success differ. For one it may be the achievement of a certain goal, a feeling of satisfaction, the attainment of a particular lifestyle, it may be a financial acquisition, or giving and contribution.

Whatever your meaning of success is, that's ok.

Despite our differing definitions of success, we all have a plan to live well. What does that mean to you? For me, living well means having adequate finances and business systems in place that allow me to travel with my husband for six months of the year whilst writing my next book or training program.

We so often think our dreams are unachievable. Though when we work backwards, and consider the true cost of the dream lifestyle we would love to have, it is often the only motivation we need to increase our hourly rates or obtain a few extra clients.

For example, you would love a commercial cleaner to come into your home every week so you can spend the extra time with your children. Okay, so you realize that for an extra fifty-five dollars per week you could achieve that. You could adjust your rates by three dollars. Book an extra hour. Or take your lunch to work. Suddenly you are easily able to afford this simple luxury. One dream achieved.

Or maybe you go to your local university and a student is willing to do the same job for twenty dollars and you are supporting a young person achieve their dreams as well. So often we compromise our dreams with negative thinking – I'll never be able to achieve that.

> If you think you can do a thing or think you can't do a thing,
> you're right.   — *Henry Ford*

Maybe you would like to travel. Plan a small trip first that will help you get organized for larger trips to come. Calculate the cost of the trip and how much you would need to set aside or earn to achieve that amount. Say it's fifty dollars a week. Determine how you could save or earn this extra income and book the trip within a month. If you plan it the finances will arrive.

The hardest step is making the first commitment to the idea and then following through by booking your ticket. In a short period of time you have become a traveller.

> Dreams pass into the reality of action. From the actions stems
> the dream again; and this interdependence produces the highest
> form of living.   — *Anais Nin*

Start with the end in mind. What's your definition of living well? What does your dream lifestyle cost? Write down the answers to these questions. Look at one dream that may be achievable this month. Use the above illustration to inspire you. Create a screensaver with images representing your dream lifestyle.

LIVING YOUR DREAM LIFESTYLE

You would be amazed how many people don't think about what they want when they consider their working life. That's why we recommend creating a wish list for your work life that encompasses personal preferences – those things that make you the happiest.

You may wish to write a novel in Tuscany. Investigate travel groups doing just that. Or maybe it is a cooking tour of Asia to add to your existing talents. Maybe you'd like to work from home or work on Wall Street.

An interesting side note is that a great personal brand will often afford the owner the luxury of mobility. What is your preference and why?

What is your ideal work lifestyle? What will your work lifestyle be like?

Working in an environment or situation that suits your personality or your personal style is important and should count high among those things you aim for. Try to visualize the ideal situation for you. List your personality/lifestyle preferences.

> If I think more about death than some other people, it is prob-ably because I love life more than they do.   — *Angelina Jolie*

When you are a successful personal brand your dream lifestyle and work lifestyle become a reality. This doesn't mean you don't work hard ... just that you have created an environment that supports your dreams and purpose as well as your preferred lifestyle.

FOLLOWING YOUR TRUE PURPOSE

The path is narrow. Be on purpose. Be on brand. Sometimes it's hard to remember that there's a purpose to your precious life.

There is an excellent scripture verse that illustrates the point perfectly. *"Because narrow is the gate and difficult is the way which leads to life, and there are few who find it"*. Matthew 7:13-14

It is very easy to be distracted from your purpose. So many people are aimlessly struggling through life wondering what it's all about. Victory is yours to claim. Seek to clarify your purpose and then disci-pline yourself to its achievement. Your focus must become laser sharp. Remain loyal to your mission and celebrate your successes and your failures, but most importantly remain true to your purpose.

It is said that all of our life experiences are aligned to our life-purpose. When we truly understand that, we will not remain stuck in the event or experience because we now understand it was for a greater purpose.

Successful brands celebrate their content and thrive when on purpose. Establishing a need to build your personal brand is essential to continually motivate you to communicate your personal brand.

OWNING YOUR DREAM

Dreaming dreams keeps us from getting stuck with the failures of the past and the mediocrity of the present. Looking forward, not looking back. It plants seeds of hope and stretches our vision. Dreaming also acknowledges that we cannot achieve everything in a week or a day. But we can plan to use the days ahead wisely. If we dream and plan to use the days ahead wisely, we can make the most of our lives.

Interestingly, the more committed you become the more refined your purpose will become. Your life-purpose may be to inspire people, transform lives.

Often your life-purpose makes sense of all the experiences you have had and what has happened to you. Our past is our definition.

Dreaming about and planning specific steps of business and personal growth creates expectancy. Each of us has a pilgrimage to complete in this life time. What is your Mecca? Jerusalem? Holy Grail? Your God has a plan for you and you are required to respond to the prompting of your spirit to accomplish those plans. You are asked to use your gifts, talents and abilities which have been entrusted to you.

We are expected to be managers and facilitators of our own dreams, not observers of others' dreams.

NARROWING YOUR FOCUS

Narrowing your focus equals power. Define your brand focus. And enhance your credibility.

This is the time to distinguish yourself as the pre-eminent source of solutions by refining your expertise. The surest way to earn credibility is by branding yourself as a "recognized" expert with an intimate knowledge of your clients, customers and industry.

Experts are sought after, get more business with less effort, and command higher fees. Experts out position their competitors because they know more and are recognized as knowing more. Give whatever you are doing and whoever you are with, the gift of your attention and expertise.

Developing a unique market niche is vital. Specialists are one hundred times more successful than generalists. Benefits of specialization include:

- differentiation – do a few things very, very well
- presumed expertise – specialization denotes expert skills in that area
- perceived value – experts demand more money
- easier to understand – more memorable, more valuable
- focus on your strengths – do a better job and make more money

It's not about being all things to all people, but being a mini-celebrity to the right people.

DISCOVERING YOUR TRUE WORTH

You have innate worth. Your life has a purpose and a plan. You have a God-given assignment and it is incredibly important that you carry out this mission.

Often personal brand growth can be crippled when people confuse self worth and net worth. It is common to see professional arrogance mingled with financial success. And conversely, people who do not recognize their innate self worth when they aren't financially successful. The other limiting belief often seen in scarcity mindsets is that financial success is achieved without ethics or integrity.

Again, the heart of this concept is the value or worth this person has placed on themselves.

Often our sense of significance is attached to our financial success or our success in fulfilling some stereotypical role. For example, a husband with several children may maintain an uneventful and financially unrewarding job for the security of earning an income for his family so the family is financially secure.

Clearly we made a choice about whether we stay in that unfulfilling role or not. Our sense of worth is deeply connected to the meaning we ascribe to remaining in that job. We may go to work each day, dying a little each day, believing that this is all that there is for us.

Or you could determine that you are building a sound foundation for your children's future and they are worth every sacrifice. Your legacy will be that they will have the ability to make better choices by being well educated, emotionally secure and responsible and caring individuals who understand work ethic and perseverance. The choice is yours. Importantly, you are a role model to your children and they are paying attention.

Steve Spielberg sent Oprah a ring and engraved on it was a quote from Schindler's List. *"Whoever saves one life saves the entire world."*

The life you save may be electing to move your children out of a drug ridden school. It could simply be encouraging your partner rather than criticizing. It could be applying tough love tactics to your boyfriend who drinks too much. Is it setting boundaries for the behavior you will tolerate? Albert Einstein said, *"Try not to become a man of success, but rather try to become a man of value."*

The question is, "What is your contribution?" You have an amazing gift to give.

PRIZING YOUR VALUE

Zig Ziglar once was questioned that his hourly rate of twenty-five thousand dollars was a lot of money for a one hour presentation. He famously responded that he was not paid for one hour, but for the thousands of hours spent perfecting his craft and researching the gems that he shared that could change your life in an instant.

A great personal brand is irresistible at any price. The added value provided to your personal brand by its brand identity is considered your brand equity.

Your reputation, your promise, your guarantee or "brand equity" is one of the few resources that you have that gives you a sustainable competitive advantage. Your reputation is an asset to be created, nurtured and used to your advantage.

You must plan your brand equity strategy and work that strategy as if your life depends on it. To accelerate the process of building personal brand equity, you must become obsessed about being intentional, hard working, and finishing everything you start.

The subtlety and power of personal branding has lead to the myth that only wealthy stars with agents and publicity machines can create a celebrity personal brand.

Consider any number of one-person industries and think how they got famous in the first place. They built their personal brand back when they weren't famous. What they had was a vision of where they wanted to go, and an instinctive understanding that to get there, they had to represent something unique and memorable in people's minds. The lesson is to start building it before we need it.

So initially, you are cultivating a strong personal brand until such time as it is a proven personal brand. Creating the kind of personal brand equity necessary to build a reputation that precedes you, takes a very, very long time. Be patient and drip feed your target market.

It takes time to have accumulated the kind of personal brand equity to make things happen. But don't equate slow progress with no progress. In a later chapter, you will consider your new or potential personal brand equity nominated as personal worth or dollar-per-hour-rate or annual income. You will be able to identify your potential brand equity simply by working through this book. Your brand equity is your new hourly rate or annual income less your old hourly rate or annual income. The balance is your brand equity.

Building personal brand equity is not a goal to be achieved. It is a commitment to a life purpose and equity is the reward for this commitment.

> Building personal brand equity is not a goal to be achieved. It is a commitment to a life purpose and equity is the reward for this commitment.
> — *Rachel Quilty*

BEING OF SERVICE

When you allow yourself to be open to your audience, your attention draws them to you. Be open to receive from your audience, their interest, their attention and even their love. Jim Rohn quite rightly said, *"Whoever renders service to many puts himself in line for greatness – great wealth, great return, great satisfaction, great reputation, and great joy."*

There is no greater satisfaction then knowing you make a difference.

PART II

Brand Yourself
Action Plan

Chapter 5

Brand Yourself Action Plan Overview

While there is no one strict method of establishing a favorable personal brand, Jump the Q®'s Momentum Formulae for Personal Branding is to purposefully and persistently deliver a positive personal performance message to your preferred market.

Building a persuasive and powerful brand cannot be achieved overnight. It is something that is nurtured over time and cannot be rushed. It is something you can, however, plan and manage easily by being prepared. Our goal is to develop an Action Plan that will prepare you for the opportunities that will now come your way as you build your profile.

To re-badge you and/or your business can be seen by some as an enormous task. And to some extent it is a big job if tackled all at once.

You are now on your own personal crusade to create a recognizable and favorable identity within your marketplace and it will now become part of your life forever. Monitoring and managing your personal brand is something that will enter your psyche and affect every activity in your future.

To establish a great personal brand, we have developed a Brand Yourself Action Plan which outlines ten Action Steps that must be completed in order to brand you for success. Your goal is to devise a Brand Yourself Action Plan and get on with it. Goals require careful, focused, thoughtful planning followed by careful, focused, thoughtful action. This chapter is about laying out the Action Steps required to play out your plan for success.

Create a Brand Planner. A loose leaf folder that you can add to and create sections within is a good start. In your planner or folder, designate a page to each of the Action Steps outlined below. You may wish to create dividers to separate the Action Steps for your convenience. Within each Action Step are several personal brand audits, questionnaires and assessment tools. You may wish to dedicate a page to various sections.

You also may wish to obtain the Brand Yourself Action Plan Work Journal to assist you record your responses to the following personal brand creation and design process. If so, go to: www.brandyourselfactionplan.com We have included case studies and video tutorials to assist you to work through the Action Plan.

Defining and designing your Personal Branding is not an exact science. It's often more intuitive, a gut feeling, a moment of clarity and point that resonates. Look for the distinction. Branding combines concepts that you've heard time and time again. If you are familiar with some of the content – look for the distinctions.

If you think to yourself -"Yes, I know that", immediately ask yourself, "But am I doing it?" If the answer is no, ask yourself "Why not?" and," What should I be working on?" Get your eye on the main game. Don't get distracted. Look for the nuances and distinctions. And implement what seems right for your brand.

As a result, it becomes vital to your personal brand's success that the following aspects of your personal brand are also clarified and relevant skills and mindset determined:

- the vision
- the mission
- the mindset
- the skill set
- the desired visual identity
- the desired lifestyle and work environment

Within later chapters, we investigate the importance of them in more detail. You will also recognize throughout this book references back to these basic ingredients in your personal brand design. Now let's review the various Action Steps to create your personal brand's Action Plan.

YOUR BRAND YOURSELF ACTION PLAN™

The ten Brand Yourself Action Steps to build a persuasive personal brand and dominate your marketplace are:

Action Step 1. Discover your existing personal brand

Action Step 2. Determine your brand's target audience

Action Step 3. Define your true personal brand

Action Step 4. Dominate your market as the authority

Action Step 5. Design your unique personal brand

Action Step 6. Develop your brand's signature style

Action Step 7. Devise your personal brand marketing plan

Action Step 8. Decide your desired outcomes, resources and skill set

Action Step 9. Deploy your personal brand message

Action Step 10. Deliver your personal brand promise

When you strategically manage expectations of your personal brand through your deliberate attributes, actions and non-actions, you become a compelling and captivating personal brand. The goal is for you to be known entirely for who you are as a person and what you stand for.

Let's briefly outline the ten Brand Yourself Action Steps and then look at them more closely in the following chapters as we work through the steps to design and build your personal brand.

Action Step 1. Discover your existing personal brand

The first step to brand yourself involves a completely honest assessment of your existing brand and to have an intimate knowledge of yourself. Sometimes to take a step forward we need to take a step back and conduct a thorough assessment or audit of the standing of your brand before revising or enhancing your personal brand.

Action Step 2. Determine your brand's target audience

To ensure you give your brand the correct focus, provide to your clients the benefits they require and meet their expectations – to do this ... you have to know who your customer is. It is equally important to determine whether you have a viable market where you can achieve both your goals as well as assist your customers in satisfying their needs and wants as well.

Action Step 3. Define your true personal brand

Personal Branding is defining your dreams and putting them into action. Your personal brand is an outer working of your life-purpose. You must pick a course and tenaciously follow it to its end.

Truly successful people who have built great personal brands dominating their niche brought a true sense of purpose to their work. And that passion is an essential part of your personal brand.

Action Step 4. Dominate your market as the authority

An important distinction to successful branding is to design your personal brand with your goal in mind. Positioning your brand as the authority or as the market-niche leader is your goal.

When you develop your Brand Yourself Action Plan through this filter or with this distinction in mind, it can promote subtle adjustments that will distinguish and differentiate your brand.

Action Step 5. Design your unique personal brand

Now that you have taken steps to define the essence of your personal brand, you have a unique point of difference. The next step is to start working on designing a personal brand that will reinforce your personal brand in the minds of your target audience until you become top of mind.

In other words, this step is about designing a personal brand that will make an impact and reinforce our authentic value in the hearts and minds of your audience. This way you are building brand equity.

Action Step 6. Develop your brand's signature style
There are many benefits to branding yourself with a signature style. Your unique style becomes an intrinsic part of your brand and differentiates you from others. You can express your brand effectively without saying a word. Your branded personal style becomes your uniform. You are always camera ready. In no time, you become instantly recognizable within your field. You become a mini celebrity in your marketplace.

It has been said that, "A celebrity is influential when she has a definable style". Individuals such as Victoria Beckham and Paris Hilton who have developed a distinct look have developed very valuable personal brands as a result. Creating a signature style is an investment in building your personal brand and leveraging your professional profile.

Action Step 7. Devise your personal brand marketing plan
To dominate your marketplace you need to implement a solid marketing plan. This is the platform from which you'll launch your personal brand goals. Marketing consists of three basic areas – publicity, advertising, and promotion.

Action Step 8. Decide your desired outcomes, resources and skill set
Each successful personal brand has invested time, money, effort and resources into themselves. Part of your brand plan for success is to develop a resource plan to aid you. You need to respect your time and purpose and request others to do so as well.

Action Step 9. Deploy your personal brand message

Businesses are continually looking for the edge. Successful communication occurs when performance matches the image. Only when you add action to words are you believed. Communication is not a neutral act; it aims for a result.

Once you know yourself, how you are differentiated from your competitors and what makes you relevant and compelling to your target audience you can define how you will communicate this unique promise of value to others. You must take charge of your strategy for success and create your own Brand Yourself Communication Plan.

Action Step 10. Deliver your personal brand promise

To brand is to promise ... and although your brand is based in authenticity, it is held in the hearts and minds of those around you.

Brands are effective because they deliver a pledge of satisfaction, quality and value. They give people something to trust and identify with. Your personal brand provides a reassuring aura that not only shows your prospect you understand their needs, but you will deliver value to them. In this Action Step we review how to keep and monitor your brand promise.

Now that you understand the mechanics of Branding Yourself let's commence your Brand Yourself Action Plan today.

Chapter 6

Action Step 1.
Discover Your Existing Personal Brand

Your goal will be to let your brand become a vehicle for your most authentic self. In this way, you'll distinguish yourself from others who do similar work, affirm your true identity, highlight your talents, and establish your reputation in business.

Reinforcing your brand and practicing brand consistency, will cause people to respond to you just as you'd like them to, so when they hear your name mentioned they make positive associations. A trusted brand earns customer loyalty. Your brand can expect the same.

So be honest, how are you currently branding yourself?

Are you:

- the "Only Choice" Brand *or*
- a Generic Brand?

When people recognize a brand name, they actually have an emotional response to the name. They know immediately what the product is. The may have confidence in its quality, or at least have an opinion about its value. We identify a product by and with its brand.

This introspective assessment will help you tap into your true power that gives you your sense of self and the personal component of your brand. Your existing personal brand is an accurate reflection of your past. They say "Your definition is defined by your past."

If you're unsure of who you are and your purpose, this provides you with the opportunity to define it.

YOUR STORY

Who are you?
What is your story?

You are the definition of your past. Who are you and how did you get here? Rely on your life's experiences to ultimately develop your inner confidence and acceptance of yourself.

An interesting past builds a solid platform for great presence, as long as that is not where you dwell.

It has been said that our life experiences are perfectly aligned to our purpose and that if we knew what God's purpose was for us it would all make sense and we wouldn't grieve our circumstances for as long as we often do.

Whatever your current or past circumstances, recognize that they are exactly the experiences you require to fulfill your purpose.

> Live out of your imagination, not your history.
> — *Stephen R. Covey*

Write out your personal story (whether or not you see it as relevant to your brand). What experiences and skills make you distinctly able to complete your life-purpose? In dot point form, catalogue your life, and experiences, highlight what you have learnt and what is uniquely you as a result.

YOUR REPUTATION

All your words and actions are sending messages to your audience, clients and colleagues. Do you know what messages you are making? Do you know what their perception is of you? If your colleagues, clients or suppliers were in a meeting today and your name came up, what are three descriptive words or adjectives you think they would use to describe you? Write these traits down.

Answer these following questions to determine your existing reputation:

- What words come to mind when people say your name?
- What do they feel when they see you?
- When your name is heard what comes into the minds of others?
- What attributes are you known by?
- What do people say about you when you are not there?
- How do other people introduce you to others?

YOUR PERSONAL BRAND SWOTT

By undertaking a simple Personal Brand SWOTT Analysis of your personal brand, you can begin to define your current brand position and commence a campaign of niche domination.

This may provide some powerful insights into your existing brand's position. It may well be the first step to rebranding, reinventing and reinvigorating your existing brand.

Your Personal Brand SWOTT Analysis includes:

- What are your personal brand's strengths?
- What are your personal brand's weaknesses?
- What are your personal brand's opportunities?
- What are your personal brand's threats?
- What are your personal brand's trends?

YOUR FIRST IMPRESSION

An excellent exercise to ascertain what first impression you make to a group is to take a small exercise book, maybe twenty pages, place your name on the cover, and circulate around the group requesting honest feedback of the individual's first impression of you.

Ensure that the comments remain confidential so honesty is fostered. Ask that any feedback positive or negative also includes an explanation of why they made that decision. To the open-minded person who is truly dedicated to growth, feedback is never negative. Remember, feedback is the breakfast of champions. Consider all feedback as constructive. This exercise helps you gain valuable insight and self perspective before beginning the process of intentionally identifying your personal brand.

Be objective about the feedback. Monitor what excuses you may make for negative feedback, how you may rationalize your first impression. It is equally important to recognize that often this initial impression can be corrected with small adjustments. For example, entering the room with a smile, taking a moment prior to entering the room to check your attitude, or simply to ensure you don't look harried and stressed.

It is important to determine and fully understand who you are and realize what messages you are communicating to others.

YOUR PERSONAL BRAND AUDIT

It is important for your growth to be able to step back and evaluate yourself as a brand.

Last Impressions
In the entertainment industry, it is said that you are only as good as your last movie or song and so it is with brand management. A poor last impression can quickly destroy a first good impression.

Never leave a customer or client feeling unappreciated or brushed off as they are likely to dwell on the experience and associate it with other previous minor misdemeanors.

Assess your online identity as well. Google® yourself today!   It's important to avoid reacting to circumstances or negative search results. It is what it is. Start driving more positive results. Review your website ranking at http://www.domainlogr.com/ to get a snapshot of your current website's brand equity.

Change negatives first

Initially, it is more important to eliminate undesirable aspects of your brand than to incorporate new behaviors. Negative traits have more power to destroy your brand than incorporating new positive traits to improve it.

It is always best to start with the things we need to change about ourselves personally – our habits, communication style and attitude. If we want to accelerate the accumulation of our personal brand equity, we must first focus on changing ourselves. All the external changes in the world will not counter a poor attitude or poor grooming. If you can master this, you will be surprised how quickly your brand accelerates.

Take an honest look at yourself and pinpoint those traits that do not support your brand. What bad habits prevent you from standing out from the crowd? If you haven't already read Brian Klemmer's book *The Compassionate Samurai*, I suggest you do. It is a great book illustrating a code of success we could all live by. Another excellent resource for unearthing our potential brand blunders is the book, *Leadership and Self Deception* by the Arbinger Institute.

An interesting aspect to human behavior is that we will behave consistently with a commitment we have made. This underlines the importance of ownership of outcomes; as well as taking the time to commit to designing and then implementing your improved personal brand.

Taking a note book and responding to the questions posed in this book is a visual and emotional commitment to achieving your desires.

Research has concluded that whenever one takes a stand that is visible to others, there arises a drive to maintain that stand in order to look like a consistent person. Make small, easy visual changes quickly to confirm this commitment to yourself and your clients.

YOUR PROFESSIONAL IMAGE

When you look good and appear comfortable with yourself your appearance can then recede from attention and others can focus on you and what you are talking about. This will focus clients on the relevancy of your products and services rather than if they want to do business with you as they consider your image.

> If a woman is poorly dressed you notice the clothes. If she is impeccably dressed you notice the women.   —*Coco Chanel*

What distractions are you offering? For example, you are a speaker and regularly receive a number of comments about your outfit. What does that mean?

Changing your professional image operates on an emotional, psychological and physical level. A professional image will generate an increased discipline and efficiency in you.

If you don't have a positive image, people will challenge your product, prices and question your service and quality. You will not be afforded the same opportunities, promotions and attention. As previously mentioned, this is called the Horn Effect.

Often your incredible potential is not recognized because your outer presentation does not endorse you. Take charge of the message you deliver.

YOUR IMAGE IN REVIEW

Subliminal Impression Components

The impression you make on others can be broken into four basic components:

Your credibility:
Your level of believability, apparent qualifications, level of intelligence, competence, trustworthiness, honesty and credibility.

Your likeability:
How likeable: endearing, affable, emotionally expressive and sociable you appear to be and how much you are like others as portrayed through your dress, behavior, voice, seniority, experience, nationality, age, sex etc.

Your personal attractiveness:
Not how slim, young or fashionable you are, but how well you manage and present yourself as you are. Great grooming and dress sense says much about your level of self-esteem, self-respect and confidence.

Your confidence:
Your apparent level of power, ability, personal assuredness and authority etc.

Use the above criteria to review the various touch points of your personal brand and review the components of your image.

Consider the way you have prioritized the brand dimensions of credibility, likeability, personal attractiveness and confidence.

If the credibility dimensions of competence and authority is of a major concern, it is wise to wear medium-dark and dark colored conservative clothing.

If likeability is more important, smile more, greet people pleasantly, wear lighter colored clothing, patterns, textured fabrics and a mix of unmatched suits are all perceived as more friendly.

Interestingly enough, the truth is you can know what people are thinking about you if you've put certain thoughts in their heads. Branding is about having a strong influence over how you're perceived.

Your Performance

Your personal brand can be critically harmed if your performance is inconsistent with your image. Identify any areas of performance which may diminish your personal or business brand.

Effective communication skills are vital to building our personal brand. Five common communications skills that you may need to review include: public speaking, rapport-building skills, asking the right questions, being a good conversationalist and perceptual agility or the ability to understand a concept and understand others' perspectives.

The public perception of a good communicator is that generally they are smarter people than those who are not as articulate.

Your Communication

Take a video of one your presentations to review your style and clarity. Make a production of it. Construct some likely questions that you would be asked and record your performance. Review the video. Analyze your presentation; your presentation speaks volumes about you. Ask yourself and some honest friends the following questions:

- What impression do I make?
- What does my body language say?
- What do my looks communicate about me?
- How do I look? Are there any areas of improvement?

Your Response to Tough Situations

Promote yourself to an expert on the situation. When you may be uncertain of what to do, ask yourself a simple question: "If I am the expert in my field, what should I do?" The answer always crystal-lizes swiftly and clearly. It may be difficult and you may be resisting.

Remember, doing the difficult thing and doing the right thing is often the same thing.

Your Mannerisms and Habits

Unprofessional drinking and drug habits let down your brand quicker than anything else. Stop it. And if you can't, seek the services of a counselor. We would say that anything that may take you off purpose could be an emotional hook.

It could be an addiction or maybe going to others' rescue; procrastination or a drama-filled life. Each of these is equally as destructive to your life and purpose as the others. If these situations persist and remain unresolved, chances are your purpose will remain unachieved.

Distractions or habits that detract from your brand, or are not congruent with your message, should be reviewed urgently.

Your Damaging Habits

You will probably find that there are only three or four habits you must change to greatly improve your personal brand. Interestingly enough, often your best attribute is also your most damaging. For example, you may be a great conversationalist, but could you get carried away and take over the entire conversation? Is your helping nature to the degree that you are taken for granted?

List your damaging habits or behaviors which if eliminated or restrained would allow you to become a more credible player in your arena.

If you pick the right habits to change, the transformation of your personal brand and corresponding personal equity can be enormous. For example, always: be prepared, arrive early, become an early riser.

Your Business Image

When people consider you and your business, what words would they use to describe it? Is this your ideal professional image and is it accurate? Does your personal brand have positive associations?

Or negative associations? Completing this exercise in your Brand Yourself Blueprint Work Journal will define your current brand position.

Does your business image

- Reflect your market's expectations?
- Powerfully reinforce your brand?
- Attract clients?
- Reflect your business goals?
- Imply your business success which includes your attire?
- Complement your brands, logos and colors?
- Reflect the culture of the business?
- Strengthen your professional effectiveness?

Your Customer Touch Points

Making a statement about your business image is at the point of each client's interaction with your business. These are known as Customer Touch Points. List the customer touch points in your business:

- office stationery
- personal appearance
- staff uniforms or attire
- marketing material
- company authoritative website
- personal authoritative website
- email signature and correspondence
- newsletter
- answering machine message
- telephone greeting
- response time and manner to client queries
- vehicles
- staff conduct and appearance
- social media forums i.e. YouTube®
- social media networks i.e. Facebook®, LinkedIn®

Consider each Customer Touch Point and what message these items say about your personal, professional and business image. Create a list of phrases that come to mind. This is step one to improving your business image. For example, you may decide that your:

- answering machine message is friendly but not business like
- newsletter is appealing but has spelling errors
- company logo is professional and clean

Is this your ideal business image and is it accurate? If not amend it quickly.

How you are perceived contributes to how people behave towards you. It is in your best interest to develop a credible and effective professional image to develop the most persuasive brand.

Your Necessary Talent

We must have a certain amount of talent to perform at the level that is expected of us. Natural ability is the starting point. The greatest brands in history identified that they had natural abilities at a young age and worked very hard and intentionally to develop those abilities to their fullest potential. Natural talent will get us started on the road to success, but if not nurtured and developed it will plateau. Often incredible talent is wasted due to the lack of discipline necessary to cultivate it.

Do the following skill set audit:

Step 1. Define the discipline you're in and specify your niche or area of specialization.

Step 2. Determine the skills that would be required to make you the authority in your field.

Areas of potential skill development may include:

- your specific discipline skills
- writing skills
- presentation skills
- selling from stage skills
- leadership skills
- management skills
- keynote speaking skills
- copywriting skills
- coaching skills
- sales skills
- closing sales skills
- public relations skills
- media skills
- motivation skills
- negotiation skills
- creativity skills
- time management skills

Step 3. Identify any skill set shortages you may have. Is it a skill you will require or is it a skill that can be outsourced?

Step 4. Once you have identified the skills that are relevant to you, select a specific skill and determine the various elements of that skill. Describe in detail what excellence looks like in each of those areas.

Step 5. Next list the resources you may need to build your skill levels in all the areas you identify. Resources may include books, training programs, qualifications, business coaches and several other types of coaches who specialize in specific areas. You can't do it alone. You must hire coaches and engage in further training programs.

Step 6. Go to work. Pursue excellence in those areas of focus relevant to your discipline. The sign of true leadership is a willingness to admit a weakness and manage it successfully. This could include outsourcing or additional training or coaching.

ADDRESS THE NEGATIVES

Fears are barriers to your success.

For example, you may fear success. What does success mean to you? You may answer, "hard work and long hours". [Note the limiting belief there, that success means hard work and long hours.] What is the problem? The problem may be that the long hours will compromise time with family and your values include that time with family is important. This is a crucial step to your success.

As wisely voiced, "A problem stated is a problem half solved."

Develop a list of internal and external fears or limitations to the success of your brand. Generally, half the battle is won just by being able to identify these limitations. You may wish to journal or do some writing around these subjects. Often times these fears have hit a nerve with your values system.

Joyce Meyer, author of *Battlefield of the Mind*, reminds us to, "Think about what you're thinking about."

Some examples of internal and external limitations (note any barriers that arise when you consider the success of your brand):

- internal limitations: self-doubt, nervous public speaker
- external limitations: transport, expense of tradeshow, lack of family support

As we move through the principles of positioning your brand as the authority, other issues may come up for you. We also look at practical methods of addressing these issues as we work through each principle. For now, just write down any limiting beliefs, limiting decisions and negative emotions. We will also consider limitations in more detail within your Brand Yourself Action Plan as we discuss the importance of your mindset on your success.

Courage is defined as taking action despite the fear. What's your biggest fear? Often the very thing you fear the most is the world you are creating.

RE-POSITIONING YOUR BRAND

Prioritize any areas of improvement with the most impact for immediate results.

These may include your email and correspondence format, email signature, answering machine message and telephone greeting so as to respond to client queries more effectively.

Your physical appearance will also have an immediate result. Always dress in your personal best colors and wear the most flattering styles for your body shape.

Adopt a "uniform" approach! Your professional image must be consistent. Use templates, stationery, scripts, systems and consistent procedures. You are quickly able to do what is required, knowing it will promote an effective business image.

YOUR PERSONAL BRAND EQUITY

In essence, you can control your bottom line, because you control the message!
It makes sense to focus and invest in areas impacting on your client's perception of you and your business. Altering your business image can be effective in capturing a greater market, building presence and ensuring long term business success.

What's your current worth: $_____/ hour? Dr John Demartini states that, "It's your self-worth that determines your self-wealth or what you'll allow yourself to be, do, and have in life."

Chapter 7

Action Step 2.
Determine Your Brand's Target Audience

To ensure you give your brand the correct focus, provide to your client's the benefits they require and meet their expectations – you have to know who your customers are. It is equally important to determine whether you have a viable market where you can achieve both your goals as well as assist your customers in satisfying their needs and wants also.

This Action Step is simply defining your target audience, their expectations and their preferences so you can satisfy them.

A successful brand satisfies two masters. The brand's owner or the corporation is one ... the brand's customers are the other. When you apply branding strategies to yourself in your career or business, you're focusing on the benefits you provide your employer; or if you're in business, your clients. This is the equivalent of meeting your customers' expectations.

Knowing your target market will make or break your personal branding campaign. Target marketing is choosing a specific audience for your personal branding campaign based on their:

- culture
- growth potential, and
- ability to generate the income they desire

These basic concepts show that the importance of correctly identifying your target audience supports the objective of your brand – to be the "only choice" brand. The goal of your brand is:

- targeting the best prospects
- developing a unique market niche
- positioning your business as the best solution
- maintaining visibility
- enhancing your credibility
- becoming the authority
- becoming the "only choice" brand

We accomplish dominance by properly defining our target market and then saturating that market with our message until we and our message are top of mind. An important part of this process is identifying a target market that we personally are congruent with.

The benefits of targeting your market are:

- higher quality target audiences
- more effective spending
- more focused messages
- less time marketing
- greater profitability
- stronger referral base
- focused efforts

Go after your target audience with a vengeance. Identify who you most need to impress and focus your attention on them. You will need a system or mechanism to deliver your message to the target audience.

Feel free to re-visit this Action Step, as over time you will continue to refine and review your target market. It is helpful to regularly assess whether your customer is still your customer and whether your demographic has changed or whether your specialty needs to be extended or changed.

Generally, before a new brand is introduced to the market a comprehensive market analysis is undertaken. You must be able to clearly articulate the answers to the following questions to direct your brand with clarity and confidence.

YOUR PROFESSION

Consider these questions:

- What do you do?
- What is your profession?
- What is your area of specialty?

YOUR GOODS AND SERVICES

- What are the goods and services you provide?
- Have you clearly defined and described your product or service?
- What are the features of the goods and services?
- What are the benefits of each of these features to this audience?

YOUR NICHE TARGET MARKET

When determining your target market or territory, think narrow. Our long-term objective should be narrow and deep. It takes a lot of courage to think and act narrowly. Don't be afraid to give up opportunity outside of your narrowly defined market. Realize that there is greater value in focusing all of your efforts within the boundaries of a distinct marketplace.

The most common mistake professionals make when defining their territory is defining it too broadly. This results in several problems:

- your message is diluted
- your resources are spread too thinly
- your mindset may be focused on scarcity

Small businesses and professionals with a brand strategy flourish by establishing themselves within a carefully selected segment of a market. They target a market niche that they can realistically hope to dominate.

What is your specialization? Who is your niche target audience?

What you call your specialty is of major importance to your brand's success in the workplace and in the marketplace at large. Aspire to become a specialist. The specialist always makes more money than the general practitioner. If your goal is to become clearly defined in who you are, so you can attract the customer or target audience you want, one way to succeed is to become a specialist.

DETERMINE YOUR TARGET AUDIENCE

Who is Your Target Audience?
Your target audience is the buyer. Knowing your audience is as important as knowing what you've got to sell.

- Who is your target audience?
- Where is your target audience?
- What do they think about your brand?
- What do you want them to think?
- How will you attract them to your product?
- Who is competing for their loyalty?
- Who will buy what you have to sell?
- Who needs to know about you so that you can achieve your goals?

Where is Your Target Audience?
Start asking yourself these questions:

- Where do I want to be influential?
- With whom does my message resonate?
- If I could pick the perfect audience, what would it look like and where would I find a high concentration of these people?
- Where can I find my target audience online?
- Where can I find my target audience offline?
- Who has my customers before me?

Do your research. The more you know, the more comfortable you're going to feel, the better a connection you'll be able to make, and the better able to pitch yourself at the right key. But remember, you still have to be yourself. Don't try to be what you're not. If it's a bad fit, it wouldn't work out anyway.

Once you know what you have to sell and have identified your target audience, finding your audience will then require a little investigation. Attend industry trade shows. Read industry journals.

Remember that what you are looking for is also looking for you. Think about where your audience is likely to be searching for you and be there.

You'll notice that when you focus on identifying your audience, you'll begin to see references, leads, and cues everywhere. If you really want to make it big, go where the action is! We have to put ourselves in the direct line of sight of our target audience. Be daring and capture their attention.

What are Your Target Audience's Needs?
Buyers are more often motivated by pain, so what solution does your product or service provide? Ask yourself these additional questions to understand your target audience more thoroughly.

- Does my target audience need my goods or services?
- Does my target audience have money?
- Will my target audience spend their money on my goods and services?
- What are their needs, wants, fears and frustrations?
- Is there a specific unmet need in the market place and who has it?
- What keeps them awake at night?
- What am I selling?
- What problem does it solve?
- What are the main reasons they will buy?
- If I could give them anything in the world, what would they want?
- What products do I sell to my target audiences?
- What other products could I sell into this niche?

Selling to Your Target Audience

What will be their objections to buying the goods and services? What could you provide to them that would prove they need this product?

Are there any value added bonuses you can provide? What do people value?

Remember, it's what they think that counts.

To successfully sell to your target audience you will need to:

- prove to them it is easy
- prove to them it works
- prove to them that they can do it
- minimize their risk
- encourage their immediate action

DETERMINE IF YOUR TARGET MARKET IS VIABLE

Ensuring your market place a viable proposition is important. It is unfortunate that many people can lose sight of the objective. Is the market sustainable? Do you have a sustainable market?

Consider the size of the market; ideally your target audience should be large enough that if you were able to capture ten percent of the total market share, you would not be able to handle all of the business that generates.

Answer the following questions:

- Are there people who have needs and wants that you can supply?
- Do these people have sufficient money to buy your goods and services?
- Will these people spend their money on these needs and wants?

Example

You may have an excellent rehabilitation program aimed at recovering addicts and alcoholics. Your heart bleeds for the unemployed and you would like to deliver your program to these people. The question you have to ask yourself is whether these people have sufficient motivation and money to purchase your program to create a sustainable business for yourself. It is possible the answer is "No".

You then have to ask yourself who has sufficient motivation and money to purchase your program. Is this an adequate market that would allow you to offer the program to others free of charge or pro bono? Are there organizations already providing services to your preferred market that you could contract to and deliver to this market? For example, you may be able to offer a workshop or session within a government funded, long-term unemployment program.

Is it something that you would be able to gift to your church who are often seeking the inexpensive service of counselors to assist their congregations? Maybe your passion and purpose could be channeled to organizations voluntarily while you maintain your existing income source.

DETERMINE YOUR TARGET AUDIENCE'S DELIVERY EXPECTATIONS

You may need to reconcile your lifestyle preferences and your target audience's expectations for delivery.

Quickly review your lifestyle preferences and your target audience's expectations for service delivery. What will you need to do to ensure they are satisfied with the promised service and products? Try and visualize the ideal situation for you!

What are your personality/lifestyle based preferences?

These are important questions to ask yourself and they will have a significant impact on the business model or workplace you elect. This in turn will impact on how you communicate to your customers and what delivery methods you will use. What will satisfy you and meet target audience expectations?

It is amazing how few people think about what they want and don't want when they consider their working life. Develop a wish list for your work life that encompasses personal preferences – what would make you the happiest?

Some things to consider:

- What type of work would you like?
- What type of work environment do you want?
- What type of people would you like to work with?
- What would you personally like to achieve?
- When or if you want to retire.
- What do you want work to be for you? To challenge you, be a breeze etc? Is it high pressure with deadlines?
- What is your wish list for the ideal work lifestyle?

The universe is waiting for you to ask for what you want.

Example

You hate to commute and your current employer insists that all staff attend work despite the hardships with public transport to get to work. You decide that in time you would like to work from home and log into your work remotely. You have a beautiful view from your windows and you have sufficient discipline to complete your work assignments competently. You now have two options. You can start researching companies who offer remote work options or discuss this with your existing employer, and maybe request a trial period.

You can see how it does not change your brand image of a hard working professional, but it does change who your target market is and what structures and boundaries you need to put in place to satisfy this employer.

If you didn't own a computer and have an internet connection, this plan may not get off the ground. However, if your files are all accessible in one file location and you have a separate office at home with a high-speed internet connection and a disciplined approach to work, you could easily sell this option even if on a one or two day per week basis, with a weekly business office meeting with your employer.

Tom Pollard of the 8020 Center has a pertinent question which addresses another lifestyle issue, *"How will I scale value delivery (how will I get the product or service to the client with decreasing dependency on your time)?"*

The key is that you can do it with decreasing dependency on your time so you can leverage your time. This could mean providing an online training program rather than a scheduled event, or it could be a group session as opposed to one-on-one consultation.

DETERMINE YOUR TARGET AUDIENCE BRAND EXPECTATIONS

Without an awareness of your existing brand and what image would ideally support your brand in the eyes of your clients, a more advanced strategy is difficult.

Your brand MUST:

- reach your target clientele
- reinforce your brand and preferred reputation
- generate trust
- have a degree of longevity and consistency

By giving you a foundational knowledge of branding and highlighting the importance of expectations and public perception, you will be able to determine what impacts your personal brand makes, and then develop simple strategies to enhance your success.

The goal is to make your first impression a powerful statement of the self-serving result your prospective target audience is going to receive from purchasing your products or services. The only reason they deal with you is that, to some extent, they see an advantage in it for themselves. They are buying a result or a benefit.

Develop a list of words you would expect your target audiences to say when they consider you and your business. Determine what values, virtues and qualities they would expect of your business. List a number of attributes, skills and talents you expect would be identified with your business e.g. leader, professional, excellence, creative.

DETERMINE YOUR PRICING STRUCTURE

What pricing structure will your marketplace accept? How do large organizations figure out what price to put on their products and services?

First, they survey all the other products in their brand's category. Then they position themselves in relation to those other products.

Some brands price themselves lower than the competition to attract a bigger customer base; others make themselves expensive and are promoted as top of the line.

The pricing structure for your products and services will have a significant impact on your branding color and design layout choices.

Customers believe they're getting the best when they pay the most, and the same is true of your customers. But do not disappoint them!

Remember how important authenticity and consistency are to your brand's success. Do not charge more for your services or ask for a salary in excess of industry averages unless you offer "value added" benefits, more than the standard product or service, and you can demonstrate it being consistently more competent, more reliable, more flexible, quicker – whatever your claim is.

Example

A target audience schedules an appointment with us at Jump the Q®. Before we even spend time with them we spend time doing an evaluation of their current branding and generate a considered report the week before the scheduled appointment.

This preparation allows Jump the Q® to generate a sound analysis of our target audience. Then we are able to competently make suggestions and provide ideas while remaining focused and informed within the consultation. It also allows us to determine whether we wish to work with that potential client and if we are able to assist them.

YOUR BRAND POSITIONING

Are your goods and services high end? Are they generic? Are they cutting edge?

Ensure your business image is branding your business and reflects your products and/or services market position. Your overall image should be consistent with your brand.

Example

As the authority in your industry ensure your business image commands your authority; whether it is a uniform, vehicle, stationery, the trappings of power or wealth consistent with your position, or as an expert in your field. People are easily swayed by the appearance of authority.

TARGET AUDIENCE'S COLOR PREFERENCES

Use colors appropriate for your target audience. For example, there are colors women like, colors men like, colors that appeal to different age groups, stereo-types and cultures.

What are the most appealing colors for your target audience?

Do those colors represent the solutions your client is looking for in your services and products? Consider which colors represent an appealing and persuasive package for your target audience.

YOUR AUDIENCE'S PREFERRED COMMUNICATION STYLE

Lesson number one in marketing your brand is to deliver a marketing message match. What, you ask?

Well, it is simple. Determine what your audience expects and deliver your message to match that expectation.

The next question to ask … is your message being delivered in the medium that best reaches your target audience? How does your target audience like to communicate? Email? Telephone? Online? Tradeshow? Regular visit?

Common types of communication may be the "Report Talk" which is typical of the way most men hold conversations. The focus is on the information.

Or a more conversational style called "Rapport Talk", the give and take style that characterizes women's conversations.

Alternatively, your niche may use slang, jargon, text talk, i.e. cu 2mro; policy and submission style, i.e. basically a lot of words saying very little; executive summary, case studies, war stories, testimonials, metaphor and parables.

What is your target audience's "talk" preference?

Your target audience also has a preference on when and how they would like to be communicated to. For example, busy executives may like emails, while people on the run will prefer a phone call and message. Others still prefer mail or invitation. Television or radio may reach your market. While a growing trend is the number accessed only online via e-Newsletters, email, video, RSS or social networking mediums.

How would your target audience like to receive communication from you? When would be the best time to contact your target audience? What is your target audience's preferred communication style and method?

Chapter 8

Action Step 3.
Define your True Personal Brand
— The Vision & the Mission

By now you know that having a personal brand is not a choice. The only choice we have is whether we want to define our own personal brand or let others decide it for us.

As a result, it becomes vital to your brand's success that the following aspects of your brand are also clarified and relevant skills and mindset determined. Within this chapter we are looking at your:

- Personal Vision
- Personal Mission

In the next two chapters, we look at the skill set and the mindset you have.

Often the difference between a good personal brand and a great one is nuance. And those who are willing to labor over the smallest details, routinely produce a more compelling personal brand. The difference between first and second place is very little. When defining your personal brand, you should always do whatever you can to refine it and make it a little bit better. Use your imagination, look for the nuance.

The following process will require you to set aside some time to truly discover who you are. Take a section at a time and work through the questions. Often it is a good idea to read over the questions and then go for a walk, run, shower or bike ride. It may be simply lying on a sofa.

When you allow your subconscious to surface and you can get extraordinary results.

This Action Step will help you identify and understand the power of your brand. Building a personal brand strategy lets us be our truest selves. Today, we are:

- waking up to our spiritual need to live authentically
- to be true to our heart's desires and their moral sensibilities
- to feel a sense of purpose and fulfillment, and
- to feel right with our path and how to navigate it

WHAT'S YOUR PERSONAL VISION STATEMENT?

A personal vision is a picture of your true self in the future. An effective personal vision includes all the important elements of your life and career. It is:

- who you want to be
- what you want to do
- how you want to feel
- what you want to own
- who you want to associate with

Although your personal vision helps you to see into the future, it must be grounded in the present. It is a statement of who you are, and who you are becoming. It is the framework for the process of creating your life.

Your personal vision statement guides your life. Your personal vision statement provides the direction necessary to guide the course of your days and the choices you make about your career. Your personal vision statement is the light shining in the darkness toward which you turn to find your way. Your personal vision statement illuminates your way.

Write your personal vision statement as the first step in focusing your life for:

- your joy
- your accomplishments
- your contribution
- your glory, and
- your legacy

Branding is a process that opens a window to the soul of the product being branded. Branding for people is about finding your "true self", who you are meant to be, who you are at your very core and putting it out in the universe to be fulfilled.

WHAT'S YOUR LIFE-PURPOSE?

I believe that we're here in the world for a purpose. Your true purpose can only be discovered when you have looked deeply and honestly into your heart and allowed the true you to be declared.

Ultimately, your business must support your life-purpose and create a congruent brand with that purpose. As a Personal Brand Strategist, my life-purpose is to nurture dreams of success. Educating people on how to create a personal brand that reflects their abilities, goals and potential allows me to nurture and encourage dreams of success and to fulfill my life-purpose.

Dr Joanna Martin, of Shift Lifestyle, maintains that the defining question is: *"If your whole life was an expression of that purpose, what would it be? Ask yourself, if you knew your God's purpose for you, what would it be?"*

We all understand that there is something bigger than ourselves that created the universe and every single one of us. We ask these questions:

- Why am I here?
- What is my purpose?

Often, we turn inward seeking answers when we should instead turn to the creator and ask these same questions. God created you with a plan and purpose. There is a reason you were put here on earth. Ask with the expectation of an answer and you will receive one.

Come up with a life-purpose statement to the best of your ability. That is what you are called to do in this life time. Remember, it is organic and will grow and evolve over time. It must be emotionally charged for you ... and put a smile on your face. For more information on finding your true purpose, see our Brand Yourself Resources section.

YOUR CORE VALUES

Your values are integral to your brand qualities. Your values are basically what are important to you. Successful brands are built on core values and during their lifetimes constantly build on and reinforce their core values.

These words identify what's deeply meaningful in your life. Use them to prompt yourself to recognize your own values. For example, are you loyal, courageous, friendly, optimistic etc?

- What do you consider to be your three or four most meaningful core values?
- When your life is ending, what will you regret not doing, seeing, or achieving?
- What are the ten things you most enjoy doing?

Be honest. These are the ten things without which your weeks, months, and years would feel incomplete.

Core values are also "essential". That is, you feel you couldn't live without them. And they are "universal", which means that they apply in all circumstances for you, all the time.

Now ask yourself these two questions:

1. How am I acting out my core values every day?
2. How am I denying my value system?

DEFINE WHO YOU ARE

Your personal brand is also shaped by your core values, passions, personal characteristics or traits, unique and signature talents and accomplishments. To build a strong brand requires a clear under-standing of your true authentic self. This means defining who you really are. Make yourself and your personality the centre of your branding.

To gain an intimate knowledge of yourself, you must have a complete understanding of:

*   who you are
*   what you believe in
*   what you stand for
*   what makes you unique
*   what you are most passionate about

Define your goals, vision, purpose, values and passions.

*   What do you stand for?
*   What are you values?
*   What are your goals?
*   What are your strengths?
*   What are some of the words you use to describe yourself?
*   What gets you in the zone?
*   What are you passionate about?
*   What makes you different?
*   What is your value?

These exercises are not about changing who you are. They are about becoming self-aware and about being honest with yourself. They require no judgments, just observations. But if you don't like what you see, it's within your power to make changes.

YOUR PERSONAL MISSION STATEMENT

Your vision is where you are headed, how you get there is your mission statement. A Personal Mission Statement is how you will manifest your Personal Vision in your daily life. It reflects your uniqueness and must speak to you powerfully about the person you are and the person you are becoming.

Your Personal Mission Statement should answer three questions:

1. What is my life about (Purpose)?
2. What do I stand for (Values)?
3. What actions do I take to manifest my Purpose and my Values?

Stephen R. Covey writes that "an empowering Mission Statement...

- Represents the deepest and best within you. It comes out of a solid connection with your deep inner life.

- Is the fulfillment of your own unique gifts. It's the expression of your unique capacity to contribute.

- Addresses and integrates the four fundamental human needs and capacities in the physical, social/emotional, mental and spiritual dimensions.

- Deals with all the significant roles in your life. It represents a lifetime balance of personal, family, work, community – whatever roles you feel are yours to fill.

- Is written to inspire you – not to impress anyone else. It communicates to you and inspires you on the most essential level."

"Creating a Personal Mission Statement will be, without question, one of the most powerful and significant things you will ever do to take leadership of your life. In it you will identify the most important roles, relationships, and things in your life – who you want to be, what you want to do, to whom and what you want of give in your life, the principles you want to anchor your life to, the legacy you want to leave. All the goals and decisions you will make in the future will be based

upon it. It's like deciding first which wall you want to lean your ladder of life against, and then beginning to climb. It will encompass – a strong source of guidance amid the stormy seas and pressing, pulling currents of your life."

Stephen R. Covey, author
The 7 Habits of Highly Effective People

Before you jump into creating a personal brand ask yourself if you can bring passion to it. You must love what you do. While your business can be successful without this, who wants to spend their life doing things they don't love.

Simply ask yourself:

- Do you have a sense of purpose for your brand?
- Are you doing what you love?
- What are you called to do?
- What is important to you?
- What's your dream?
- What's your big idea?

If you never had to work another day in your life, how would you spend your time instead of working?

YOUR PASSION

What gets you out of bed in the morning?

What really makes you happy? What do you love to do? What are you passionate about? Who you are can be inferred from the things that interest you most. These may overlap with some of your values. Values have an inner significance, and passions are more "of the world."

Make a record of those things you love most. It doesn't matter how many items are on your list. Some people have many different passions. Or you maybe someone who has only one grand passion!

Branding gives you the opportunity to become brand NEW! This process is the foundation work that will guarantee you stability and success. Of all the things you might succeed at, those things you're passionate about give you the best possible chance for success.

DETERMINE YOUR CRUSADE

What do you stand for?

What's your contribution? For example, Oprah once said that, "The greatest contribution you can make to women's rights, to civil rights, is to be the absolute … best at what you do."

Are there any common threads among the words you can list as your passions? Do any of your passions exist in your present work or in work you're considering moving into?

> I stand for freedom of expression, doing what you believe in, and going after your dreams.   — *Madonna Ciccone*

YOUR CHARACTER

Create a thorough list of all aspects of your character. Describe everything about who you are as a human being. Do not be modest. Use fulsome superlatives to describe who you are. Your list should be very complimentary. Your list could include components of your intellect, personality, background, education, likes, quirks and interests.

A further exercise which can add to your list is to consider a time you felt you were at your best. Close your eyes and record your observations and later write them down. As you do, notice all of the positive qualities you observe in yourself.

You may want to highlight your brains or intellect, charisma, sex, fashion sense. Create a list from your visualization. Then move to another scenario and continue to build your list.

To ensure your list is truly an accurate reflection of who you are, beside your list of qualities provide an example that is evidence of this quality.

Next group the qualities together that would make your target audience feel more strongly about you. When you have completed this list, note the benefit of these collective qualities beside them.

Once you have reviewed and received some constructive feedback on your benefits, select the benefit that you will build your brand upon. Remember, you can only choose one. Trust your instincts. Select the one that resonates with you the most and is most relevant to your target market.

So ... what's your keyword or benefit that you would like to build your personal brand around?

CREATE A CAUSE

What is your brand's objective? Personal branding is really about defining your dreams and putting them into action. Your brand's objectives may be threefold – how your brand will help your clients, the planet and yourself.

I mention the planet in a more philanthropic manner of how are you helping the planet, Mother Nature or others. It may be that you maintain a paperless office, buy renewable products, deliver a carbon neutral office, that you offset your business's footprint.

Alternatively, you may aid a charity with time or donations or tithe to your church. If you don't have the time or resources to commit to a charity, no doubt your church will have plenty of worthwhile causes that would appreciate your contributions.

Importantly, this contribution, in whatever manner you choose, will invoke the law of reciprocity. Give and you shall receive. Sow and you will reap. Give with the expectation that you will be rewarded for your giving and you will be. There is a phrase I have heard that sums the situation up well, "don't hope and pray – believe and receive."

Do you approach your business with higher goals in mind: to educate, to serve the community, to help people etc?

YOUR BRAND PURPOSE

Ask yourself, "What is the purpose of my brand? How can I help or support others? How will I know if I have been a successful brand?"

Before you jump into creating a personal brand ask yourself if you can bring passion to it. You must love what you do. While your business can be successful without this, who wants to spend their life doing things they don't love?

Simply, do you have a sense of purpose for your brand? Ask yourself:

- Am I doing what I love?
- What am I called to do?
- What is important to me?
- What's my dream?
- What's my big idea?
- What do I want to be?
- What am I knowledgeable about?
- What solutions do I provide?
- Do I know exactly what I can offer?

If you never had to work another day in your life, how would you spend your time instead of working?

YOUR DREAM LIFESTYLE

Assume you have built the perfect business for you. Consider the following questions about it and the lifestyle it creates for you:

- What income will you have?
- How many hours a week will you work?
- How many staff will you have?
- Where will you live?
- How much will you travel and where?
- What will you own?
- How will you spend most of your time?

Unfortunately, it is not uncommon for people to struggle in some kind of job for which they have no passion, and which doesn't in any way reflect or complement their personal values.

When creating a successful brand for your work life, aim to incorporate both your values and your passions in what you do and how you conduct your business.

KNOW WHAT YOU'RE NOT

Often, clarity can be achieved by considering what you and your brand are not.

Knowing what you are and are not can save you a lot of resources because you can focus your communication and attention.

Personal boundaries are an absolute necessity for keeping yourself and your brand distinguished.

LIST YOUR SUCCESSES AND CHARACTER BUILDING FAILURES

If you wish to be a speaker, a key element to your presentation is to obtain permission for your presence on stage. This entails a brief overview of your history which has assisted you gain the authority and expertise to competently address the topic of your presentation.

To position ourselves as an authority in our field, we have to have a proven track record of excellence to position. We can easily overlook our achievements and not grasp their significance to our brand, unless we review them.

**LIST ALL THE SUCCESSES OF YOUR LIFE
FROM CHILDHOOD TO NOW.**

Sometimes, we are blind to the positive outcomes of a challenge or problem we have endured. Recognize that every experience you have had is aligned to your purpose and each event or failure has had a purpose of building your character to prepare you for your life-purpose and ultimately your most authentic brand.

List all the areas that may be perceived as negative in your life, the challenges and obstacles that you have overcome and identify the positive outcomes that have resulted from these situations.

Consider what positive and negative aspects of your life have given you the ability to position yourself as someone of merit in your field of expertise.

Create a personal history that chronicles the events that have had a relevant impact on your brand.

CONSIDER YOURSELF AS A BRAND

If you were a product, what would you be? What are you, and why? Spend some time thinking of a brand you can identify with.

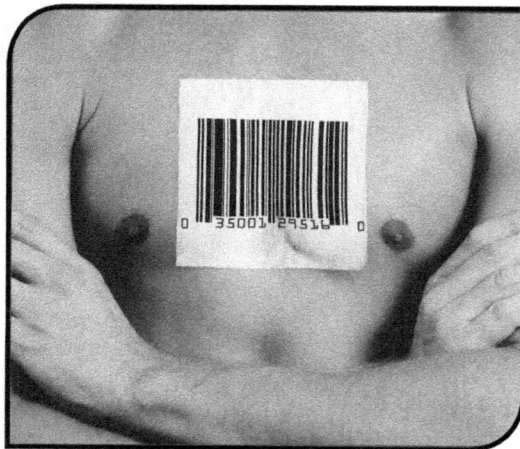

Now consider, are you a food product? Are you an appliance? Are you a fashion item? When you've thought of a brand whose description seems to fit you personally, try substituting your name for the brand name. Can you claim the same about yourself in real life?

You should think in the most positive terms about yourself. Branding is positive by nature. It will bring out the best in you.

Another good exercise is to consider which of these items best reflects who you are. Identify what items or thing best describes you and why.

- If you were a car, what car would you be and why?
- If you were an animal, which animal would you be and why?
- If you were a female celebrity, which celebrity would you be and why?
- If you were a male celebrity, which celebrity would you be and why?
- If you were a building, which building would you be and why?

If the brand you chose doesn't describe you accurately, keep trying. Find a brand that suits you better. By working at it, these exercises will reveal some of your essential ingredients, which we'll use to customize your brand description later.

YOUR PERSONAL TAGLINE

When you think of how to describe your brand, look for something you can deliver consistently. If what you put out there is truly you, this won't be a problem. Your description may be a paragraph long, however, that is a lot for people to remember. Your tagline is the verbal equivalent of a logo that will come to people's minds when they hear your name. It is a capsule description of who you are, what you do or your benefit to clients.

Edit your definition down to a sound bite and hook it to your job or career.

Maybe people will give you a tagline. Ensure it is a tagline that supports your brand or truly represents your brand and you are happy to maintain it. Alternatively, start moving to tag yourself and adjust the message.

When selecting our personal brand tagline, we might decide that we want it to relate to an aspect of our physicality. For example, Arnold Schwarzenegger is *The Terminator*, Dwayne Johnson is *The Rock*.

Is there a catchy phrase that you would like to be known by?

YOUR BRAND TAGLINE

Taglines are benefit-driven, inspirational, or descriptive. They say what the consumer will get from the product, or what the product hopes to achieve, or they define the product.

Investigate your competitor's taglines so you can differentiate yourself. Then think of your values, passions and talents. Your tagline may take inspiration from there. Try to specifically incorporate some of your key benefits or attributes in the line, in words that will set you apart. Your challenge is to capture the essence of what you have to offer, create interest and enthusiasm for it and enhance your image in the business world.

This time instead of describing yourself as a personality, describe yourself as a professional. Your tagline should be a clear, concise declaration of who you are and what you do. Let's consider some well known taglines:

- Nike - Just do it
- L'Oreal - Because you're worth it
- Apple - Think Different
- Elvis - King of Rock and Roll
- Michael Jackson – King of Pop

Be specific and be creative. Don't brand yourself a raw food dieti-cian; like Jenni Snook, call yourself a Raw Food Genie, and feature your specializations within that theme. Maybe like James Schramko, Internet Marketer, you get "Super Fast Results". Develop a tagline for both yourself and your business and use them with all promotional opportunities.

Your tagline should have longevity and be memorable. Robin Fisher Roffer in her book *Make a Name for Yourself,* suggests, "Take plenty of time developing this important word picture for yourself. How will it look as a kind of caption for your name? How will you feel about being referred to and remembered this way?"

YOUR MOTTO

We often have life mottos running through our head that may or may not serve us. What phrases do you use often? What do you regularly say when something goes wrong? What do you say to yourself when things are going right? Check your language. Identify these state-ments and make a note to yourself to consider them later with other beliefs you may have.

It's important to consider these words and phrases carefully, while they may sound good, they need to be relevant to the needs of the target audience.

YOUR FAVORITE QUOTES

What's your life quote? What's your favorite bible passage? Do you think that a strange question? Miley Cyrus and Paris Hilton wouldn't agree with you. Recently, Oprah asked Miley her favorite verse in the Bible and Miley easily quoted the verse that had special meaning to her. She was consistent with her brand. It is well known that Miley Cyrus has strong Christian beliefs.

On the other hand, when asked shortly after her incarceration, Paris could not quote a favorite verse. Surprisingly, she had claimed her faith had got her through. Clearly, the media questioned this comment with a quick test of her Bible knowledge.

As your brand and success rise, you may be asked the same question. If not a Bible verse, than what is your favorite quote? People will question you on how you achieved your success, being able to quote an interesting or famous quote often illustrates your point.

In preparation for your own celebrity within your field of endeavor, it may be important and wise to have some quotes documented and memorized that you can incorporate into your message. Developing quotes around your field is also a great idea, as editors and journalists seek to include comments and quotes. Being able to quickly extract a quote from your website is a great way to develop brand exposure.

Vision, commitment and faith can make a brand successful. But strategic purpose, planning and preparation will make it great.

THE MEANING OF YOUR NAME

In the Jewish culture they believe your name is a prophetic utterance of your true nature. Hence, they changed their names as they grew or changed in nature. I strongly feel that our name is a true indication of our purpose, or the manner in which we are to fulfill our purpose. If you are concerned about the meaning or character of your name, look for a deeper meaning than just the superficial meaning.

Are you being true to your name?

Chapter 9

Action Step 3.
Define your True Personal Brand
— The Skill Set

YOUR PERSONAL BRAND ATTRIBUTES

By answering the following questions, you will get an excellent over-view of your personal brand attributes.

- What does your brand do?
- What are the best things about it?
- What do you want people to think when they hear your brand?
- What reputation do you want your brand to develop?
- What benefits do you provide your target audience?
- What are your distinguishing qualities?
- What are your brand's key attributes?
- What are your brand's defining characteristics?

These qualities must resonate with who you are and what you stand for.

- What words come to mind when people say your name?
- What do people feel when they see you?

Branding is about having a strong influence over how you're perceived. Think Volvo, think safety. Think Nike, think *"Just Do It"*. When applying brand promotion to people you get similar results. For instance, what words come to mind when you think of Richard Branson? Madonna? Oprah?

All these people have powerful personal brands. Their names evoke a strong, even emotional response from us, and we pretty much know what to expect from each of them, which is why we remember them. They're consistent.

Consistency is one of branding's most important principles. Richard and Oprah build their brands by making career choices that reinforce what they're known for. Brand inconsistency is critical to developing brand loyalty. Brand inconsistency erodes confidence. Unless that is your brand, Madonna and Lady Gaga would be a good of example of a brand being consistently inconsistent. This type of brand is high maintenance.

Donald, Richard, Madonna and Oprah have created their own personal successes in just the same way any other successful brand does – by focusing on who they are and what is unique about them, on who they want to reach and how they want to be thought of, and by packaging and promoting themselves to accomplish their goals.

Your brand's success is achieved in the same way. The very first step is to model your brand on your authentic self. There's only one brand like it in the world, which makes it distinct from any other and something you and only you can pull off.

An interesting exercise is to write a testimonial to yourself from a pretend client. Make it big and glossy. Ideally, your testimonial should answer these questions. This would also be an excellent method to obtain valuable testimonials from your existing clients in the future. Ask these questions of yourself as the client, and of your existing clients:

- What were the results I achieved from these products and services?
- What concerns did I have that these products and services helped me with?
- What were my expectations of these products and services? Did I have any particular emotional reactions to these products and services?

- How will these products and services help me
  in my day to day life?
- How did these products or services change my life?

YOUR GIFTS AND TALENTS

Your talents and skills are also an important part of your brand's distinguishing features. So ask yourself what you are really good at. Don't limit yourself to qualities that only seem career related.

By the time we're adults, most of us know a few things we do well. But we may be overlooking talents that have fallen by the way-side. Think back to when you were a child.

- What did your parents or teachers praise you for?
- What were your favorite subjects at school?
- What extracurricular activities did you like best after school?

Ask others to tell you what each of them thinks is your foremost talent. Write down what they tell you.

I often ask clients what is in their life that's lingering in the background and just won't go away. Is there a quiet passion or interest that has rested in your thoughts and activities for some time?

This is valuable brand information that usually reveals something deeper than the skills you may already be aware of. This information is very valuable.

- What are your work related skills and talents?
- What do you bring to the table?

Ask your friends and family, your new branding focus group, to consider your list of work-related attributes. If you can count any of these among your talents you may want to emphasize them in your brand description.

Identify your attributes that are prized in the workplace. They may be that you are a good listener, efficient, good communicator, dedicated etc.

In business, these attributes are as much an expression of talent as the ability to play the piano. They are distinguishing characteristics prized by employers, clients and the general public. They may be counted among your "key attributes" as part of the distinguishing characteristics of your brand.

If you're a natural in any of these areas, you might not even be aware you are distinguished by them. Discovering what others think are your best distinguishing features can be very educational. Often, we sell ourselves short.

Add those words that speak of your unique brand qualities – your values, your passions, your special skills – and make a record of five key attributes that you want to accentuate to your audience.

We also have aptitudes and capabilities that haven't been noticed by others or by us. One of the ways we can uncover these is by trying new things. And when you discover what resonates with your soul, trust it. The process is more than just finding your talents – you have to honor your talents, too.

To help you uncover your hidden talents, I recommend trying two or three new things a year.

YOUR AREA OF FOCUS

Kaplan Mobray, author of The 10Ks of Personal Branding delivers a powerful tip on defining your personal brand focus. He asks the questions:

- What in your life have you been most deliberate about?
- What has been the outcome of your deliberate focus?
- What is your personal brand's area of deliberate focus?

YOUR SPECIAL SOMETHING

What you call your specialty is of major importance to your brand's success in the workplace and in the marketplace at large. Aspire to become a specialist. The specialist always makes more money than the general practitioner. If your goal is to become clearly defined in who you are so you can attract the customer or client or audience you want, one way to succeed is to become a specialist.

Your area of expertise – your specialty – doesn't have to be an art or science. It may be a factor of your personality or one of your prized attributes.

From these values, passions and talents you possess that have money making potential, narrow your focus to an area that you can develop as your niche or specialty.

Important questions to ask are:

- How do I intend to profit from my brand?
- How will I know if my brand has been successful?
- What would I have achieved?

It's crucial to be specific about your goals, and to record them in a way that's measurable, so you can evaluate how effectively your brand strategy is working year to year.

As is often the case, your personal success may be reflected in your financial success. However, as I tell every client, our definitions of success differ. For one it may be the achievement of a certain goal, a feeling of satisfaction, a particular lifestyle, it may be financial acquisition, or giving and contributing. Whatever your definition of success is, it does need to be clearly identified.

What do you dare aspire to?

For simplicity we use a dollar figure as a measure of value or worth.

When we consider the worth of individuals and the value that others would attribute to brands such as Mother Theresa or Martin Luther King, we would ascribe a nearly priceless value.

As highlighted in the movie *Schindler's List* *"To save one life is to save a world".* And I often tell the story of the farmer who helped a neighbor's son, and the neighbor was so grateful that the neighbor paid for the farmer's son to go to school. The neighbor's son was Winston Churchill and the farmer's son was to become the man responsible for the discovery of penicillin. Our purpose may not be to be known by millions around the world or to save millions but to facilitate those whose purpose it is. Whether we are the farmer or the neighbor's son or Mother Theresa or Martin Luther King we all have an important job to perform.

So, we can ask now, "What is the value of the farmer or the neighbor?"

Wasn't their role equally important? Whether in the slums of India saving a few desperately hungry individuals at a time or on Capitol Hill sharing a dream to hundreds of thousands, their equal significance, worth and ultimate value to humanity is indisputable.

You may be the farmer or the neighbor's son.

We look more closely at the skill set your brand will require to accelerate its growth in later chapters. At present, it is an excellent benchmark to record our existing abilities, skills and talents. This will also allow us to recognize our strengths and to obtain resources in the areas that we may need assistance.

Chapter 10

Action Step 3.
Define your True Personal Brand
— The Mindset

YOUR MINDSET

When you decided to build your personal brand you joined the top one to five percent of high achievers in the world. This is where you allow the real you, the real person you're meant to be to come out. Often when addressing your mindset around personal branding, issues of fear, doubt and worth arise. Therefore, we need to look at what blockages may exist to your success.

> Knowing others is intelligence; knowing yourself is true wisdom.
> Mastering others is strength; mastering yourself is true power.
> — *Tao Te Ching*

Often when you set a goal and apply an extremely positive filter, self doubt and objections, and internal conflicts arise. For example, you might hear this voice say: "You could never be the industry leader.', "You don't deserve it.", "Self promotion is vain.", "You're not good enough.", "You don't have the knowledge, skill, drive etc to achieve this ...".

Alternatively, fears of success, fears of failure, fear of rejection may arise. Negative emotions may arise at yourself and others for allowing yourself to stray from your path for so long.

There are decisions or beliefs that you may have made at some time which maybe preventing you from accelerating quickly and easily in order to achieve your greatest good and your best personal brand. These issues are very revealing and may need to be adjusted in order for you to advance rapidly.

Bill Cosby has said, "In order to succeed, your desire for success should be greater than your fear of failure."

We have entered a new era, where we are increasingly recognizing the manifestation of Rhonda Byrne's "The Secret" philosophy – the law of attraction. And through the personal development explosion happening right now, we are discovering that we are largely responsible for the results in our world.

Essentially, we have created the life we are leading. Whilst this is challenging, it is immensely empowering. We can take charge of our lives. We can make changes as difficult as they may seem. Personal responsibility is something we all agree others should have, but we struggle to maintain it ourselves.

While we have looked at the positive aspects of your abilities, attributes and attitudes, the quickest way to change your life is to remove the negative aspects first.

- Were the results you achieved satisfactory?
- Were you content with your life and its outcomes?
- Are you completely happy with your current situation?

To some degree we must all be content to be discontent, to continually improve our lives.

We have all had a problem that we've really struggled with. Consider your mentors and decide who would be the best person to discuss the situation with, who will insist you acknowledge your personal responsibilities within the situation, and make it someone who will hold you to account for your actions and insist you honor your word.

To solve any problem, here are three questions to ask yourself:

1. What could I do?
2. What could I read?
3. Who could I ask?

My multi-millionaire mentors, Andrew and Daryl Grant, of *Our Internet Secrets* asked me to consider the following concepts and questions. I share them with you to assist you on your personal branding journey. To become extremely successful or wealthy you will at some point need to address your mindset. This is a great place to start.

As you move into your future, you need to focus on who you are as this new person. To move into the future you need to change you. The old you cannot exist in the future. You need to do things differently. To be in the top one to five percent of your field you need to sacrifice your existing comfort zone and ineffective habits and attributes.

Does a top athlete in his field make sacrifices? Does he experience pain?

If you want to be a top athlete or the authority in your industry or the leading expert in your field or take your present success to the next level, you will need to make some sacrifices and experience some pain.

The important aspect of maintaining the right mind set is to focus on the new person. Ask yourself these questions:

- What does my new life look like?
- What does the new me look like?
- What mindset, skills and abilities does this new person have?

To become this new person, we must also look at the person you were and recognize that old behaviors, habits, mindset and relationships may not support the new you. We look at this aspect of your personal brand more closely in Action Step 8. Decide your desired outcomes, resources and skill set.

There will be challenges that you need to address. You may need to change old beliefs, habits and old relationships. Rather than continuing to suppress the pain by covering it with old habits and behaviors, focus on who you are as a new person. What would that new person do?

Identify those old behaviors; habits, thoughts and relationships that do not support the new you fully or which are causing you pain or frustration. What are those things in your current life that challenge the success of your new life and the new person you wish to become?

Ask yourself these questions:

- What is the area of pain I need to address?
- What will I do with these old behaviors; habits, thoughts now?
- What am I going to do?
- What would the new person do?

In regards to your relationships, ask:

- Will I comply with the old dynamics of a relationship?
- What will I do for each of these relationships?
- What am I prepared to give these people?
- What are the new guidelines and boundaries I will put in place?

Draw up a set of new guidelines for each relationship.

Remember, your subconscious will challenge you and test your resolution.

Personal branding involves an honest assessment or brand audit to identify areas of improvement and to acknowledge our own mistakes. Apologize or accept and then move forward. Personal branding takes responsibility and is willing to admit mistakes and correct its faults and errors upfront.

Are you taking responsibility for the person you chose to be?

We are so quick to justify our motives. We are quick to deflect criticism. We are quick to find fault. And, we are quick to lay blame on others, usually our spouses, children, colleagues or bosses.

That is why often the next set of questions are the hardest ones you are ever likely to experience. But they are also the most powerful in your personal growth. So here goes. Take heart. God would not have put you on this path if he didn't think you were good enough or worthy of his plan or didn't have the ability and fortitude to achieve it.

Ask yourself:

- Are there any old habits or relationships that need to be reviewed again?
- What will I do with these relationships or habits?
- Will I comply with the old dynamics of a relationship? Or will I set new guidelines and boundaries?
- What behavior will I accept?
- What would that new person do?

When defining your goals for your personal brand, you may have a little voice in your head heckling you. This is when you question your right to expect these outcomes or results.

It is important to recognize the voice and identify the beliefs behind that suggestion and question them.

EXAMPLE

One of your brand goals is to earn $300,000 per year. If you have never developed a sense of personal financial potential or even considered yourself able to be self sufficient, you may hear a voice saying you're not worth it or you're not good enough. Or any number of other suggestions.

It is good when a limiting belief comes up so you can address it. Get a picture in your mind of when you may have made this decision, "that you are not good enough or not worth it", now look over it and determine what you were meant to learn from that situation. These should be positive lessons you were meant to obtain as a result of that experience.

I've found that when we think of ourselves as "brands" and work at increasing our product value in the marketplace, it practically guarantees a major boost to self esteem because it is a positive, proactive process, and because it gets results.

After all Michelangelo once said, *"The greater danger for most of us is not that our aim is too high and we miss it, but that it is too low and we hit it."*

Ask yourself:

"Why build my personal brand? If I had a fantastic personal brand what would I do, be or have?"

or

"It is important to me to build a fabulous personal brand because ..."

Listen to any voices or suggestions that detract from this positive outcome. Identify any fears and limiting decisions that arise.

Struggling with who you really are and whether you deserve your desired outcomes? Write a love letter to yourself. Every one of us should be in a healthy love affair with ourselves. We should care so much about ourselves that we are constantly looking for ways to improve, nurture and grow.

YOU'RE OVERCOMING OBSTACLES

Robin Fisher Roffer, author of Make A Name For Yourself, offers the concept of creating a contingency plan for working through your identified limitations or barriers. She recommends that you, "Use this three-part system to identify and work through obstacles that stand in the way of [your] career success.

    a.   Record the potential obstacle
    b.   Make a promise that is a solution to the obstacle
    a.   Take steps to support the promise

For example:

    a.   **Obstacle:** My tendency to rise late
    b.   **Promise:** I will wake up at 6am
    c.   **Steps:**

        1.   Set my alarm
        2.   Go to bed earlier

Make a habit to be at my desk fifteen minutes prior to my usual starting time.

Go back to Action Step 1 and review and determine how you can overcome any obstacles you identified there.

YOUR COPING STRATEGIES

Studies have shown indisputably that reading and listening to motivational books and programs releases endorphins and dopamine into the blood stream which provides us with a sense of well being. It's not a coincidence that people with the best personal brands also have the most positive and optimistic outlook on life.

For example, your coping strategy may be exercise or it may be watching a movie. Psychologists recommend different movies for different reasons. For example, if you are feeling down, watch "*Pay It Forward*", if you are confronted with a perceived glass ceiling, watch "*GI Jane*", if you need a reminder that we all make mistakes, watch "*Top Gun*" or "*Iron Man 2*".

Don't wait till there is a problem to determine you're coping strategies when things get tough. Decide today what you would like to do.

YOUR ABILITY TO BOUNCE BACK

Without a doubt, the most enduring attribute a personal brand can and should have is an ability to bounce back. It has been said that your level of success is related to how high you bounce back up after a failure. Recognizing that a failure offers a clean slate and affords a re-calibration of your brand, let's consider how we can learn from our mistakes. If done with intent, this process can become an advanced branding strategy, see case study below.

> Even a mistake may turn out to be the one thing necessary to a worthwhile achievement.   — Henry Ford

Often a bounce back allows you to appeal to a wide audience. Recent events in the lives of Britney Spears and Tiger Woods are a testimony to this. Their brands became world famous, extending out of their previous demographic. The world as voyeurs caught a glimpse of the real person behind the manufactured brand. To some extent, finally seeing an authentic person, an audience may be more forgiving and find the brand more appealing for a number of reasons.

For most people, without the entourage and PR machine that can be whipped up at a moment's notice, we need to consider these bounce back basics about coping with the ups and downs of life."

The three steps to bouncing back are:

1. grieve about your failure for 24 hours
    i.e. cry/punch the wall/vent etc
2. next, move on by acknowledging all your current
    and past successes, then
3. analyze and learn from the failure and turn it into
    a positive experience

Some tend to jump straight to Step 2 or Step 3, and other people don't. Don't assume you or other people aren't coping with the failure when they react as per Step 1. That is part of the process and some can move more quickly than others onto the next step. Everybody develops different coping mechanisms for failure and we need to support each other and ourselves as we work through those processes rather than judge ourselves or others too harshly.

We are our own harshest critic. When a failure occurs as it will inevitably, take the time to work through the steps at your own pace. Be forgiving of yourself. You are human after all. A negative will only remain a negative if we don't learn from it. Know that you are on the road to success and realize that failure is merely a detour.

As Henry Ford said, *"Failure is simply the opportunity to begin again, this time more intelligently."* The only difference between a good day and a bad day is which one we choose.

Case Study: Brand Bounce – Fashion Police cite Obama

Well, you would think that the world had better things to talk about than the US President's jeans. But no – the whole world tuned into the discussion.

It would be easy to mistakenly think we were discussing the complex DNA molecular structure that makes Obama unique and how this man came from nowhere to become the leader of the free world. Nothing so academic, in fact we're discussing the jeans he wore to bowl the first pitch of the Baseball World Cup 2009.

Now, while some people may disregard this as gossip magazine fodder, branding and marketing experts were delighted to witness this first inconsistency in the brand call "Obama".

We witnessed an important branding lesson. What the fashion police labeled as "grannies pants" and a huge faux pas, some branding experts identified as a simple branding mistake. A brand with sufficient goodwill can overcome this misstep.

Lesson number one in branding is to deliver a marketing message match. What, you ask?

Well, it is simple. Determine what your audience expects and deliver your message to match that expectation.

When we think of President Obama, we may think polished, articulate, well groomed and professional. When we consider Obama's well worn, ill fitted old jeans, we receive a different message. We get an incongruent picture to what we would have expected. Our mind begins to question which message is correct. Our brand is questioned.

In the minds of millions, Obama had failed to maintain his personal brand.

Everyone makes mistakes, it doesn't matter how good they are. A person's ability to recover from mistakes depends on firstly, how you respond to the crisis or mistake and secondly, the amount of goodwill you have generated or built up.

In this case, significant goodwill was present for the mishap to be forgiven. Let's look at the lessons we can learn from this situation.

Lesson for beginners: Don't disregard your appearance, even if it is a relaxed event. This can be a trap for the unsuspecting at a conference or attending a business social event. Always be well dressed and maintain your image to be consistent with that of your professional image. Ensure your wardrobe supports your personal and professional image at all times. And, always wear great well fitted, new jeans to sports events especially if you are going to have millions tuning in to witness your wardrobe mishaps.

Now, for the advanced strategy: Branding Strategists would appreciate a superior re-calibration strategy at play. During this period of the Presidency, observers were tagging Obama as more interested in the celebrity of the Presidency than tackling the state of the economy.

This wardrobe mishap afforded the President an opportunity to advise the population he was not interested in fashion and being seen in the most polished outfits, he could not afford the time and energy, he had a country to run. In an arena where you don't move unless its planned, most brand strategist would applaud this move as a master stroke to correct and re-calibrate an existing brand and re-establish the correct brand message.

Chapter 11

Action Step 4.
Dominate Your Market as The Authority

Get ready to stake your claim as "the" authority in your industry and position your brand as the "only choice" brand when you follow the principles outlined below.

One of the biggest mistakes people and brand strategists alike make with personal branding is creating a personal brand without a true intention.

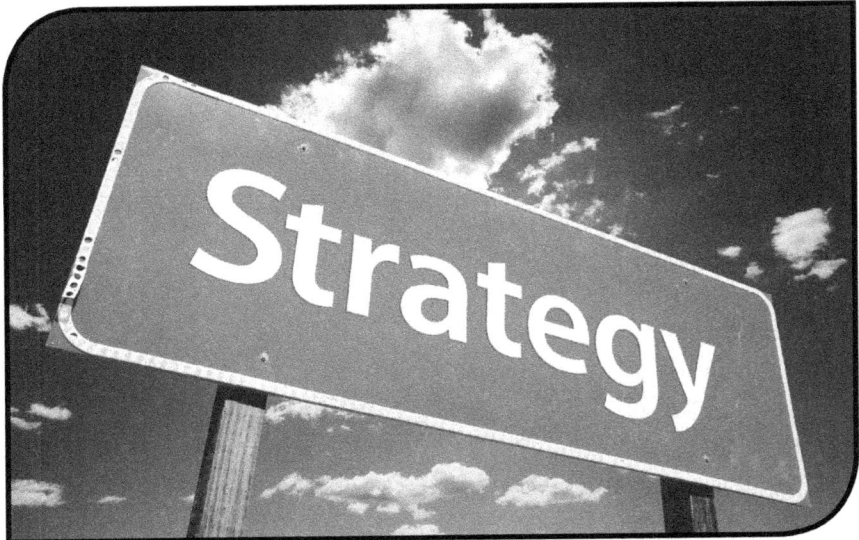

The purpose of branding yourself is to differentiate yourself, and achieve the desired result of being known as the thought leader or "the" authority in your field. An important distinction to successful branding is to design your personal brand with your goal in mind.

Positioning your brand as "the" authority or as the market- niche leader is our goal.

When you develop your **Brand Yourself Action Plan** through this filter or with this distinction in mind, it can promote subtle adjust-ments that will distinguish and differentiate your brand.

Imagine that you are creating a business brand for a professional accounting firm. The concepts you may use include smart, profes-sional, crisp and appropriate. **Now**, imagine creating a business brand for the leading accounting firm in the country. Would your branding step up a notch, become more cutting edge and promote a new level of attention to detail? Absolutely! Therefore, it is important to review and create your branding through this filter and positioning as "the" authority.

Notice we intentionally use the term "the authority" not "an authority". Anyone can become an authority on a subject. Our goal is to create your personal brand as the "only choice" brand – "the" authority.

The principles of positioning yourself as the AUTHORITY in your industry include:

A = Attributes
U = Unique
T = Territory
H = Hook
O = Opportunity
R = Reliability
I = Image
T = Trustworthy
Y = Yourself

When continuing the next several Action Steps, adjust your branding to your new positioning within your industry. Let's discuss each principle in turn.

A = ATTRIBUTES

Napoleon Hill once said, "People buy personality and ideas before they buy products and services."

Your Brand Personality Strategy

Your Brand Personality strategy is a strategy that showcases your personality and equates it with your personal brand to produce an emotional bond with your prospects or target audience. This puts the human touch into your business by bringing your personality to the forefront of your marketing and business entity.

What do people value? Research into tipping has revealed that larger tips do not co-relate to efficient and prompt service. Instead people tip more when the staff make them feel good. We pay more for small gestures of friendship.

The closer the brand personality is to the consumer personality or the one they admire and aspire to, the greater the willingness to buy the brand, and the deeper the brand loyalty. This means you need to match your personal branding strategy as closely as possible to the overall predisposition of your target market.

What are your most favorable attributes to emphasize as part of your personal brand? What is the best positive personality to support your brand?

In many studies questioning thousands of clients, when asked why they purchased products or services from the top sales performers, inevitably that person was described as "nice". Whoever has the most likeable personal brand has the best chance of winning.

Interestingly, talent is not enough. You have to have the discipline to create a more likeable brand to get ahead.

According to a Harvard Business School study, a person's likeability is more important than skills when it comes to getting hired or promoted, despite managers' claims to the contrary. Talent matters less than perception does. The ability to work is a given. The quality of the work is a given. A personal brand is what makes us unique.

Attitude matters: Attitude sells

Consider Ellen DeGeneres, Steve Irwin, and Richard Branson – all incredible individuals with enormous wealth, but loved because they are or were nice people, great down-to-earth people. True to themselves, the same in real life as they are portrayed to be in the media.

Be Emotionally Attractive

Make yourself emotionally attractive. Good things happen to those who are emotionally attractive. The word or phrase we choose for ourselves should in some way reflect the emotions we want to evoke in our target audiences. For example, when we think of Volvo we think of safety. It makes sense that Volvo has a safety conscious culture and safety is incorporated into every aspect of their business.

In life and business things go wrong; if you are a nice person people will be more tolerant of a mistake. Small flaws are overlooked, because of the goodwill generated by your personal brand. If you're known as a nice person, this causes other people to want to know you.

Likeability and visibility bring you riches, access, opportunity, influence and freedom.

Have Empathy

Empathy is also an attribute evident in most great personal brands. Empathy is the ability to feel what others feel and to let them know it. It means that you are really listening to people because you are genuinely interested in them. You are curious about who the other person is, what they are thinking and feeling and why they think and feel the way they do.

The most charismatic people in the world have a way of making people feel important. Their success is the product of one skill: their ability to pay attention. The master at rapport is able to build a conversation on other people's level and terms. They also ask intelligent and engaging questions.

Ask yourself ...

- What are your most favorable attributes to emphasize as part of your personal brand?
- What is the best positive personality to support your brand?

U = UNIQUE

Our personal brand is about who we are personally as opposed to what we do for a living. To choose an authentic personal brand that represents the value or quality we want others to think of when they think of us.

- How do your express yourself in a unique way?
- What is distinctive about you?

This can be a gift, a signature or the manner in which you dress. It must be something that distinguishes you. What makes you unique is likely to make you successful.

Your personal brand is the word or phrase we want others to think of when they think of you. One of the most successful examples of this is illustrated with the huge success of the pop group – Spice Girls. Individually each girl was different enough to be easily identifiable. That difference proved to be an ace for the Spice Girls. In 1996, the Spice Girls became known as: Scary, Ginger, Baby, Sporty and Posh. Victoria Beckham, as Posh Spice launched not only a music career but the eventual enormous personal Beckham brand estimated to be worth over $250 million.

A decade later and following the final act of Spice Girls in 2000, Victoria "Posh" Beckham is still a major media and business force.

Posh – meaning smart, rich or fashionable, exclusive; all accurately describe Victoria. Today Victoria Beckham and posh are synonyms. The Beckham brand is emulated in the term "'posh" – smart, rich, fashionable, and exclusive.

When you think of the industry leaders in your field ... what word or phrase comes to mind when you think of that individual?

How would you like to command the same degree of respect and influence with your target audience? The key to achieving such success is building a great personal brand and marketing that brand better than your competition.

When confronted with the challenge of selecting from several good choices, the next strategy your target audience looks for is unique-ness. Be unique. Command attention! Differentiate yourself from your competition.

- What is unique about you?
- What unique attributes do you possess which distinguish your personal brand?

As Seth Godin promotes in his book, *Purple Cow*, *"You must be remarkable – you must be a Purple Cow."* You must be unique and distinctive to survive in tomorrow's marketplace.

T = TERRITORY

The best positioning you can have among your prospects and customers is that of the expert, the authority in your area of expertise.

- What's your personal brand's territory?
- What one area of specialization will be the most helpful to your brand?
- What's your market niche? Or market micro niche?
- What's your specialization?
- What's your topic or area of deliberate focus?

Focus your brand on an area of achievement.

- What one area of specialization will be the most helpful to your brand?
- Is it customer service, is it product knowledge?

What are you special at? Focus your brand on one area of deliberate focus.

Become A Specialist

What you call your specialty is of major importance to your brand's success in the workplace and in the marketplace at large. Aspire to become a specialist.

The specialist always makes more money than the general practitioner. If your goal is to become clearly defined in who you are so you can attract the customer, client or audience you want, one way to succeed is to become a specialist.

Some people, such as Sales Guru Brian Tracy, say that if you read twenty books on any one subject, you're an expert or a specialist. Becoming a specialist is essential for the clear identification of your brand. You will stand out in the sea of lost generalists.

Your objective is to find out what makes your target audience feel good and then give it to them in the form of your personal brand.

As a specialist or as a consultant, your customers look to you to give them valuable advice they can use to improve their work or life in a cost effective way. When you walk, talk and act like a specialist or consultant; you set yourself apart from people who see themselves as salespeople. You begin moving into the top ten percent in your field.

Here are several methods to brand "you" as a recognized expert:

- publish articles in trade publications
- get interviewed
- give talks at groups comprised of your prospects
- take a leadership role in networking organizations
- host special events and invite prospects
- package your expertise into books, seminars and information products

Define Your Micro Niche

Your territory is also your micro niche target audience. Defining your micro niche clearly targets your best prospects.

In many sales orientated businesses, a sales representative may be responsible for the sales and customer contact in a certain geographical region. However, your territory is not necessarily restricted to a specific area, rather to a specific micro niche target audience.

Tom Pollard, CEO and Strategic Marketer of the 80:20 Center, describes your micro niche, for example, as selling "black jelly beans" and your target audience the people who love black jelly beans.

What's your black jelly bean?

H= HOOK

To produce results, visibility must be combined with credibility. This means that you need to embrace visibility strategies that display your distinction, competence, expertise, authority and leadership. A hook is a term used in journalism, which represents an issue that makes a story "newsworthy". To be newsworthy, your personal brand must have a hook.

Having a hook means, your personal brand should be one or more of the following:

- Be memorable, for the right reasons
- Be visible and attention grabbing
- Be seen. Repeatedly and consistently
- Be there. Just showing up to commitments can build your brand
- Be known. Often people will give a referral for no reason other than they are known
- Be involved. Attend networking functions, go on committees
- Be grateful. Send thank you notes
- Be reactive. Take advantage of topical issues and respond quickly
- Be irresistible. Focus and listen to others
- Be charismatic. Give your undivided attention
- Be heard. Have an opinion on current affairs
- Be active. Contribute to forums and social media sites
- Be proactive. Distribute articles and press releases
- Be focused. Become a specialist in your field
- Be committed. Follow up and keep promises
- Be passionate. Have enthusiasm
- Be disciplined
- Be stylish
- Be confident
- Be optimistic
- Be someone
- Be different. Creativity elevates you above your competitors
- Be true to your brand
- Be "On" Brand

In her book, *Confessions of an Heiress*, Paris Hilton advises, *"Put yourself on your own pedestal and then everybody else will, too. Always act like you're on camera, and the spotlights are on you. Always behave like you are the center of attention."* I love it!

Keep in mind most people will firstly judge you by what you wear, then how you speak, then the words you say. Always be memorable for the right reasons. Personal branding has nothing to do with what you think about yourself and everything to do with what your target audience feels about you.

Never believe that your output, resume, work performance is of more value than your appearance and your personal appeal. Remember, it may be a person's appearance that captures your attention, but it's their personality that captures your heart.

O = OPPORTUNITY

Master the art of connection. Get involved. Being everywhere brings great opportunities. Don't wait to start connecting and promoting yourself and your personal brand. Perfectionism will sabotage you.

Start today and:

- think like the industry leader or an heiress
- take the opportunity to take a lead role
- take advantage of opportunities, say yes and then figure it out
- think like a marketer and tap into trends
- create your own opportunities

Sometimes people fail to realize that a great personal brand does not drive circumstances, as much as circumstances create opportunity for great brands to emerge. Consider the personal brands of Winston Churchill, Paris Hilton, and New York City Mayor Rudolph "Rudy" Giuliani.

Find Opportunities

Great personal brands enjoy the power of the pull. Pull is when your reputation precedes you to the point that others seek you out and pull you forward. With a great personal brand opportunity finds you.

Opportunity is afforded to those who take a leadership role in the personal brand development. Many people are provided opportunities which they don't take advantage of. Taking advantage of an opportunity can be as simple as returning a phone call, creating an article when requested, providing a gift voucher or responding promptly to emails.

In an interview with Julia Roberts of *Pretty Woman* fame, Oprah said of Julia's comment on being lucky, that "Luck [or success] is when opportunity meets preparation."

Determine that you want to be the best in your field. What are the best in your field doing better than you or that you are not doing? Identify what opportunities may be being afforded to others and make similar plans to create opportunities elsewhere.

Beware of Treadmill Behavior
Beware of engaging in treadmill behavior that prevents you from proactively seeking out and taking advantage of opportunities. At the end of the day, we are responsible for our own results.

Ask yourself:

- Why haven't I already taken advantage of existing opportunities?
- Why aren't I creating opportunities?

Add your responses to your list of limitations in Action Step 3. Define your True Brand - Mindset.

The objective of personal branding is to become the "only choice" brand of choice, the recognized leader and authority within your industry. Leadership is independent of formal positions. No one gives you power, you just assume it.

Generally, we cannot buy or pester our way into the highest circles or incredible opportunities – we have to be invited. However, more importantly when we are invited we better have something special to offer.

Conversely, be prepared to turn down opportunities that may potentially dilute your focus from your target market.

Remember, your goal is not attention but glory. Glory is fame with honor. Being famous is not hard. Becoming famous for the right reasons is a little more challenging.

R = RELIABILITY

Great personal brands are built through alignment and congruency of the personal brand and the person's day to day activities and actions. For our personal brand to have influence, we must live it day in and day out in everything we do and say.

A truly great brand separates itself from the pack by paying attention to the little details that most others either overlook or don't care to pay attention to.

- be someone who can be relied on
- treat everyone the same and always be the same
- your public behavior should always be consistent with your private behavior

Be congruent. Treat everyone the same and always be the same. People largely accept you, at least initially, at your own evaluation of yourself.

In other words, whatever you say about yourself, however you describe yourself, people will accept without argument. They will then watch your behavior to make sure that what you say about yourself and the way you behave are consistent with each other.

Brian Tracy, Sales Guru, frequently discusses the need to be congruent and consistent in your personal and public life. Importantly, if you are not consistent and aligned with your personal brand eventually this will be seen.

I = IMAGE

Personal Branding is the art of self-packaging. You are the message.

Ask yourself some questions.

- Do you dress and look like a first class professional, in every respect, when you go to work, and when you meet with your customers or suppliers?
- Are you proud of the appearance of your staff?
- Do you feel happy to introduce your staff, with the way they currently dress and look on the outside, to your customers and suppliers?
- Are your offices neat, clean, organized and attractive?
- Are you proud to have critical customers visit you and walk around your facilities?

One reason why image is so important is that, when you look absolutely excellent in a personal or business situation, you feel absolutely excellent as well.

When surveyed, three in four Americans (seventy-five percent) said that a person's appearance on the job is likely to affect whether they are taken seriously. Eighty-four percent of women and sixty-eight percent of men agreed with the statement.

When you dress like a winner, you think, feel and act like a winner. Most people do not know how to dress for success. It pays to design your image to sell. The way you look is a reflection of you and how your product or service works.

If you look good, your product or service will be good, and your prices justified. It is well known that more presentable, well groomed, attractive or professional people are more persuasive. You need to develop a highly effective professional image thus creating credibility.

Learn the secrets to packaging your brand. Create a visual identity. A signature look will distinguish you from the crowd. In Action Step 6, Develop Your Brand's Signature Style we outline the essential ingredients to creating a signature style.

Investing in your brand image is investing in your future success.

- What are the best in your field doing that you are not?
- What are the best doing better than you?
- How are they dressed?

Develop a consistent image or look, a signature style. A coordinated, consistent and professional image becomes your signature. Style is about projecting an accurate sense of yourself and your business.

The way you look on the outside can help you or hurt you. Your appearance is an important success factor, and can contribute immensely to your luck. Sometimes, your image can make or break you in a critical business relationship.

Your Clothes

If you work for a salary, dress the same way the people two jobs above you dress. Spend twice as much on your clothes and buy half as many. If you are a junior clerk, come to the office looking like a junior executive. You will immediately attract the attention of people who can help you.

Aim to look sleek and professional, someone who looks like they've come to work, to work! If you want your income to go up invest in your appearance and that means good quality clothes that fit perfectly.

Three main rules to follow when building your professional wardrobe:

Firstly, your appearance must project that you are confident, reliable and competent in your current position.

Secondly, your dress should emulate those who hold the position one or two positions above you.

Thirdly, pay attention and maintain the most polished appearance you can, at all times. Little things say a lot and can sabotage your professional image very quickly.

Get the attention you deserve with these simple steps:

- Know the colors that look great on you. Before you purchase an outfit ensure it complements your skin tone, eyes and hair color.
- Wear clothes that are flattering for your body shape or physique.
- Choosing the right styles will make you look taller and younger.
- Choose accessories that complement your outfits.
- Bring the whole look together with your hairstyle and grooming.
- Your image should reflect your brand identity and personality
- Create a smart image with a winning smile and attitude.

Everything counts – you are either building your brand or weakening it – the choice is yours. Never believe that your output is of more value than your appearance. Dressing smartly solidifies your professionalism and will add momentum to your career.

As I say ... if you're going to make an appearance – make it the right one.

Finally, how could you develop the habits of walking, talking, dressing, working and behaving in such a way that others describe you in the most positive and flattering way.

Your image and grooming are a direct reflection on you.

- Do you care about yourself?
- Are you disciplined?
- Do you pay attention to detail?

T = TRUSTWORTHY

Our personal brand is our promise to people about what they can expect from us in the way of results. Start thinking about what promise you want to deliver to your target audience.

Is it expertise? Trust? Quality? Professionalism? Make your selection carefully because once you pick your promise and build a reputation, it will be very hard to change.

The real power lies in our having the courage to stand for values or qualities that truly reflect who we are as opposed to who we think our target audience wants us to be.

Make your promise singular. The best brands are simple, straight forward and unambiguous. The objective is to become synonymous with a single quality or trait.

Pick one thing and be known for that one thing. The aim is to become the epitome of that value or quality.

Integrity basically means – what you think ... is what you say and what you do. Your personal brand's perceived quality or "Trustmark" is simply, a promise to the customer.

When you think Volvo, you think safety. When you think Nike, you think *"Just Do It"*. The fact that you remember the brand name and have positive associations with that brand makes your product selection easier, and enhances the value and satisfaction you get from the product.

Your personal brand is importantly a reflection of your values and those of your target market. A customer's purchase or buying decision is based on what is important to them and what they value. If safety is important, you may consider purchasing a Volvo given its reputation and the value it places on safety.

A good brand name gives a good first impression, is easy to remember, and evokes positive associations with the brand. Be optimistic. People "buy" optimists because they enjoy their company. People "buy" people with integrity because people with integrity do what they say they will. People with integrity can be relied upon. Trust opens doors.

Your brand is your promise. Ask yourself these questions:

- Do I keep my personal promises?
- Do I honor my word?
- Do I keep my personal brand promises?

Ensure your brand is congruent with your personal values. Your brand should denote excellence or a high quality. Does it build your credibility?

Follow up religiously! The secret to a persuasive brand is execution – do what you were hired or engaged to do, do what you promised to do.

Y = YOURSELF

Be yourself. Be authentic. Authenticity begins with a true acceptance of the real you. Choosing a personal brand that is not a true reflection of the real you is dangerous and high maintenance. You will feel like a prisoner and you will be discovered.

If you feel under pressure when you are on brand, review whether this is truly your best personal brand. Your personal brand must be "a true reflection of the real you."

When selecting our personal brand, we must look at ourselves through the eyes of our target audience and never lose sight of what they see and how what they see makes them feel about us. This is an easy principle to acknowledge, but a difficult one to practice.

We need to be absolutely honest with our assessment of ourselves because if we are not honest, we will have great difficulty identifying the personal brand that is right for us.

Do Not Violate This Rule
Whatever part of our character we promote, this is one golden rule we must never violate. We must never try to be something we are not.

You are your own PR Department. Your brand should:

- identify you as the authority
- command authority
- position you uniquely
- deliver on promises made
- reinforce your values

Stephen R. Covey, summed up being authentic well, *"In the last analysis, what we are communicates far more eloquently than anything we say or do"*.

Be your own brand. Be on brand in all that you do. Don't follow trends, or fads.

As Judy Garland once said, *"Always be a first rate version of yourself instead of a second rate version of someone else"*.

Chapter 12

Action Step 5.
Design Your Unique Personal Brand

YOUR PERSONAL BRAND IDENTITY & STYLE GUIDE

A major element of your personal brand is your Personal Brand Identity. Your personal brand identity is made up of your:

- brand name
- brand associations
- messages
- image
- environment
- symbolism

Identity is fact ... the effective sum of the facts that can be used, in the minds of various audiences, to distinguish a given entity from all others. To manage our personal brand identity is to manage these facts.

Now that you have taken steps to define the essence of your person brand, you have a unique point of difference. The next step is to start working on designing a personal brand that will reinforce your personal brand in the minds of your target audience as the "only choice" brand. In other words, this step is designing a personal brand that will make an impact and reinforce your authentic value in the hearts and minds of your audience.

Your brand and your image are basically the same thing – it's how you are perceived by others. And as we see from the above essential elements of successful brand management, without a clear direction or purpose the end experience of your brand may not be the one you wish to be identified with.

It makes sense to focus and invest in areas impacting on your personal brand identity. Altering your personal brand identity can be effective in capturing a greater market, building presence and ensuring long term business success. In essence, you can control the facts about your personal brand and distinguish you from all others.

The following issues should also be considered when planning your new personal brand. Does your personal brand identity:

- reflect your market's expectations
- powerfully reinforce your brand
- attract clients
- reflect your business goals
- and attire imply your business success
- indicate it is complemented by your brands, logos and colors
- reflect the culture of your business
- strengthen your professional effectiveness

Develop the habit of thinking continually about how you are positioned in the hearts and minds of your clients, how you are being branded.

BRAND YOURSELF STYLE GUIDE

Our Brand Yourself Style Guide will help you further develop your personal brand identity. Your Personal Brand Style Guide progressively encapsulates all your brand elements including your personal brand:

- value statement
- vision statement
- mission statement
- strategic plan
- promise
- culture
- theme
- unique value statement
- uniqueness statement
- success standards
- audience statement
- business model and style
- ideal work lifestyle
- personal brand personality
- archetype
- target audience communication preferences
- color strategy
- online branding, including your personal domain
- signature customer touch point
- signature ritual
- signature theme song

Once you have designed your personal brand identity and created a Personal Brand Style Guide you can start rebadging your brand. Use the following brand identity implementation checklist to ensure your new brand is evident on all your customer touch points.

YOUR PERSONAL BRAND VALUE STATEMENT

Your brand value statement acts as your roadmap to success. Defining your brand is creating a simple brand positioning statement. Value statements are simply an acknowledgment of the inherent worth of your personal brand and the products and services you produce. Value statements are usually brief and to the point.

The goal is for you to be known entirely for who you are as a person and what you stand for. Establish yourself as [Name], a [Insert specialty here] who is known for [Insert your unique perspective].

YOUR PERSONAL BRAND VISION STATEMENT

The vision statement, by contrast, is not about what your personal brand currently is, but what your personal brand hopes to become. As an example, a vision statement may acknowledge that your personal brand already meets industry standards in customer support, while at the same time setting goals for moving customer care to a higher level within a given time period.

The vision statement is a form of value statement. A vision statement is intended to be no more than a couple of sentences that clearly outlines a specific goal of your personal brand, while not providing the details of how that goal will be reached. Thus, the vision statement provides the direction for your personal brand, while not inhibiting the development of the strategy that will allow your personal brand to reach that lofty goal.

YOUR MISSION STATEMENT

A mission statement is more concerned with the overall aim of your personal brand. It's a simple statement of your personal brand's reason for being. Often the statement will make a pledge to deliver a superior product or service to customers on a consistent basis. From this perspective, a mission statement is about maintaining a certain quality or attribute.

Every person or business that stands behind a brand has a "mission", which communicates the brand's soul and its purpose in life. To help define your brand's purpose, and to keep it uppermost in your consciousness, develop a "mission statement" based on your personal brand's objectives for its products and services.

The mission statement acts like an affirmation and motivational tool for you and your branding guidelines. The mission statement expresses your highest ideals on behalf of your brand. Your mission statement wants to be a self-fulfilling prophecy.

Your mission statement should resonate with your core values and express your higher ideals. Try to articulate your mission statement in ten words or less. It will be easier to remember that way, and you want to be able to think of it easily, like you would a motto, when you need to be reminded of who you are and what you stand for. Put your mission statement up on your office wall.

YOUR PERSONAL BRAND STRATEGIC PLAN

Plan the strategic aspects of your new personal brand. A strategic plan is a disciplined, coordinated, systematic, and sustained effort that enables an organization to fulfill its mission and achieve its vision. A strategic plan generally covers a five year rolling time-frame. It links the mission to the vision.

Strategic plans are reviewed annually to monitor progress and ensure alignment with other planning cycles. It establishes imperatives, goals, strategies, and performance measures for the organization that can be used as a management and communications tool.

The following strategies are to achieve your personal brand goal to enhance your personal brand awareness. A strategy is an integral part of your strategic plan. A strategy is the plan of action, method, process, or specific step taken to accomplish a goal in a strategic plan. They indicate how results will be achieved. Each goal and objective will have one or more strategies.

YOUR PERSONAL BRAND PROMISE

The promise is the expectation you've given your market members over time. It's what you want to be remembered for. It's your uniqueness. It's how you differentiate your brand from your competitors. It's what gets the attention of buyers. It's what generates desire and invokes favorable emotions.

What is your brand promise?

YOUR PERSONAL BRAND CULTURE

What's your brand culture? What's your way of life? Does that reflect in your business, work environment, and customer touch point? What is the soul of your company?

The best example I have seen of this is within the Virgin Group. The overall brand culture is fun. We see this in almost every aspect of the Virgin Group businesses from staff announcements in-flight to credit card terms and conditions. Give yourself permission to take your brand culture into your work environment.

Another excellent example of culture is seen in the Australian Dream Centre Christian Church, where their culture is to perform acts of random kindness (Ark) to show God's love through acts of love, charity and community works. This culture has generated an incredible following where you become an "Arkoholic" and "Ark" people. The "Arkee" then goes to www.arkd.info to describe how they were "Ark'd".

YOUR UNIQUE VALUE STATEMENT

Uncover your unique promise of value and develop your unique value proposition or statement. What's your elevator pitch? Create and memorize your personal fifteen second commercial, aka the elevator pitch. This should be a concise, articulate value statement. Consider a phrase you can comfortably live with and grow with and you'll always have a great response when asked, "What do you do?"

One of the best methods to build powerful brand equity is the fifteen second commercial. Ensure you are better than your competition by articulating your message in a way that captures people's attention. Paint a compelling, technicolor word-picture of who you are.

Your elevator pitch should explain:

- Who you are
- What you do
- What benefits you provide
- What unique value you provide

YOUR UNIQUENESS STATEMENT

Yes, it is very different to your fifteen second commercial. It is the response to your audience's next question, "How are you different to everyone else?" What is your brand story? What differentiates you from your competitors and peers?

What's the one thing you do better than all your competitors? Determine that you want to be the best in your field. What are the best in your field doing that you are not doing ... or are doing better than you? What's your point of difference? What difference do you make?

YOUR SUCCESS STANDARDS

Create a code of excellence or success standards that outlines your expectations about behavior, attitude and performance which you will adhere to. The book "How to Master Your Traits" by Bob Borg is an excellent reference to draw from, as it highlights the twelve most prevalent character traits of successful historical figures.

These are rules you commit to live by on a daily basis in order to elevate your game to the next level. To create these rules, imagine you have achieved the "Only Choice" status. What rules would you live by? What rules did you live by to achieve that success?

YOUR PERSONAL BRAND AUDIENCE STATEMENT

The other side of "What does my target audience think of me?" is the question, "What do I want them to think about me?" A successful brand is where the two have the same response.

Stand in the shoes of your target audience and ask yourself, "What do I want them to say about me?" Create a mock testimonial or Audience Statement. Writing down these positive statements, commits you to fulfilling them.

This is the performance standard you should now hold your personal brand to.

YOUR BUSINESS MODEL & STYLE

Your personal branding is very dependent on your business style, business model, and pricing structure. Your business style or wealth creation style plays to your strengths. Everyone has a primary wealth creation style. For example, are you the Landlord, Property Developer, Buy and Hold, Buy and Sell Quickly, Builder, Designer, Dealer or Property Manager? See Recommended Reading List for further information. What is your wealth creation style or business style?

This will have a direct impact on your business model selection. Select a business model that supports your business style and your target market's preferred model. What's your best business model?

Consider the pricing structure for your products and services. This will have a significant impact on your branding color and design layout choices. White space gives an appearance of quality and establishes subliminally a higher price bracket in the audience's mind. While busy space, more crammed with information, gives the impression of lesser quality and lower costs.

What's your pricing policy and pricing structure?

The psychology behind a format, brochure layout, merchandising display or stand is incredibly important to understand. Hotspots attract your audience's attention. For example, copywriters will tell you that an image in the top left corner is a good sales tactic as a picture tells a thousand words and we all look to the top left. It is a fascinating science that should be part of your investigations in the future.

What's your best format, brochure layout, merchandising display or stand?

YOUR IDEAL WORK LIFESTYLE

Read Tim Ferriss's book, *The 4 Hour Work Week*, to really give you a great idea of what you can achieve for a work lifestyle.

What is your ideal work lifestyle? What will your work lifestyle be like?

YOUR PERSONAL BRAND PERSONALITY

What is your personal brand personality style? Your brand should embody the word.

Narelle Todd, Successful Living's CEO and Chief Professional Organizer, once recommended that you plan your life consistently with your personal style. Plan your life to be consistent with how you recharge your batteries. Planning your work environment and customer touch points should be no different. They should reflect your personal style and promote your core values.

Identify your personal descriptive qualities and then clarify the benefits those qualities provide your audience. Pick one benefit upon which to build your personal brand. And if appropriate, turn that benefit into a catchy phrase.

Define what you are really selling to your client. The bottom line is that if you want your personal brand to sell, it must offer your target audience something your target audience wants. Whatever you select, your ambition should be to become the epitome of that quality.

The more authentic the choice, the more vivid the images will be in your target audience's mind and thus the stronger their emotions will be.

YOUR BRAND ARCHETYPE

Anyone who's delved deep into traditional business branding has probably run into the concept of "brand archetypes," popularized by Margaret Mark and Carol Pearson in the book *The Hero and The Outlaw: Building Extraordinary Brands Through the Power of Archetypes*. You can use the Jungian Archetypes or the following "22 Universal Brand Types" in your brand creation and your brand positioning strategy.

For example, are you a Maverick - a Rebel, an Outlaw, or a Rogue? Brands such as Harley Davidson, Virgin, MTV, Rimmel and Steve Madden are themed around this archetype as are the personal brands of Henry David Thoreau, Sid Vicious, and George Washington. Generally, their goal or method is to achieve freedom from the establishment through defiance, disobedience, and nonconformity.

Let's look at the following archetypes:

- maverick (rebel, outlaw, rogue)
- everyman (good old boy, girl next door, average Joe)
- innocent (saint, goody-two-shoes, angel)
- entertainer (clown, jester, performer)
- villain (bad guy, monster, vampire)
- intellectual (sage, genius, expert)
- sensualist (hedonist, pleasure seeker)
- servant (martyr, slave, monk)
- traditionalist (conservative, old school, miser)
- nurturer (mom, mother earth, healer)
- connector (networker, politician, talker)
- artist (creative, creator, craftsman)
- philosopher (sage, prophet, guru)
- dreamer (magician, sorcerer, wizard)
- motivator (mentor, preacher, promoter)
- ruler (king, leader, father)
- explorer (seeker, wanderer)
- defender (knight, superhero, warrior)
- thrill-seeker (gambler, swashbuckler, adventurer)
- achiever (athlete, hot shot, strongman)
- underdog (struggles against overwhelming odds)
- lover (helps people feel attractive, special, belonging, and worthy of love)

Consider the traditional branding archetypes above; which category do you fall into? Do any of the above archetypes align with your brand?

YOUR PERSONAL BRAND STYLE GUIDE

Style Guides offer you the chance to present your Personal Brand Identity in a consistent way. They help to ensure one tone is used for all branding. And they help save time and resource by providing an instant answer when questions arise about preferred style.

A style guide document that details recommended usage of graphic elements designed to create a uniform look across promotional materials and websites, establishes best practices for use of logos, typography, colors and layout in order to develop brand equity through visual consistency.

In short it is a document that:

- clearly defines the rules and standards of how a logo and accompanying branding elements should be used
- sets out the ground rules to follow with a logo so that the business' corporate identity system is adhered to
- sets out standards for design and writing of documents, either for general use or for a specific publication or organization

Our objective is to create a comprehensive Personal Brand Style Guide for your brand. Your Personal Brand Style Guide would address the following:

- brand name:
- brand attributes:
- brand identity:
- brand color palette:
- brand fonts:
- brand typeface:
- brand formatting:
- brand logo:
- brand imagery:
- brand theme:

- business brand name:
- business tag line:
- brand description:
- key attributes:
- values:

Your Personal Brand Style Guide would address the following:

- personal brand attributes:
- personality/attitude:
- personal brand summary:
- personal brand profile:
- personal tag line:
- personal title:
- personal brand story:
- personal brand promise:

Your Brand Signature Style Guide may address the following:

- packaging:
- presentation:
- brand power:
- positioning:
- bottom line:
- quote:
- brand culture:
- what people think of:
- what people are missing:
- define your brand community:
- define your fan club mentality:
- relevant psychology:
- relevant astrology:
- relevant numerology:

Add to and extend the above Style Guide to encapsulate any branding elements you would like specifically addressed.

YOUR BRAND COLOR STRATEGY

Color has an immediate psychological impact. Choose the color and design of your stationery, logo and uniforms with care. Some colors build rapport and credibility immediately. Ensure your business considers the psychological effects of color. While perceptions of color are somewhat subjective, there are some color effects that have universal meaning. Colors in the red area of the color spectrum are known as warm colors and include red, orange and yellow. These warm colors evoke emotions ranging from feelings of warmth and comfort to feelings of anger and hostility.

Colors on the blue side of the spectrum are known as cool colors and include blue, purple and green. These colors are often described as calm, but can also call to mind feelings of sadness or indifference.

Use appropriate colors for your target audience. For example, there are colors women like, colors men like, colors that appeal to different age groups, stereotypes and cultures. What are the most appealing colors for your target audience?

Do those colors represent the solutions your client is looking for in your services and products? Consider which colors represent an appealing and persuasive package for your target audience.

When the onlooker's brain picks up contrast (color difference) it literally comes to attention, and results in the person being remembered, listened to and taken notice of. Color contrast is a vital factor in impression management:

- high contrast (bright, dark combinations)
- medium contrast (light, dark combinations) – this is the most people-friendly and professional level of contrast
- low contrast (little or no color difference between the garments) - this is a combination seen as elegant, but in business it may create a forgettable, boring and ineffectual appearance

Determine which colors and color contrast is best for your brand and aligned to your target audience.

YOUR TARGET AUDIENCE COMMUNICATION PREFERENCES

What is your target audiences "talk" preference? Is it "report talk" or "rapport talk"? Alternatively, your niche may use a slang, jargon, text talk, i.e. cu 2mro; policy and submission style, i.e. basically a lot of words saying very little; executive summary, case studies, war stories, testimonials, metaphor and parables.

Your target audience also has a preference on when and how they would like to be communicated to. How would your target audience like to receive communication from you? When would be the best time to contact your target audience?

Ensure you design your brand around the preferences of your target audience.

YOUR PERSONAL BRAND THEME

Can your brand be developed around a theme? Your theme may be a movie, show, book, iconic characters such as Coco Chanel, James Dean; famous or well known groups such as Samurai or the Mafia, sports such as boxing, wrestling.

For example: Jump the Q®'s Personal Branding services are themed around the movie industry. I am the Director of Dreams. I am a talent scout. My clients are the talent. And my clients become the movie stars. I can move in any genre where my talent (client) excels. I facilitate and manage the final cut. Our team looks something like this:

- Graphic and website designers - Production team
- Stylists, make up and wardrobe - Professional Image team
- Copywriting, Internet marketing experts
  – Online Marketing team
- PR machine, Agent, Publicist, Media contacts – Public Relations team

YOUR ONLINE BRANDING

Capture your personal brand identity elements in your:

- corporate authority website – When visiting a client or going to an interview, take your laptop and show them your website, specific interests and/or services
- personal blog website – Your personal blog should be similar to a personal scrapbook appropriate to share with your professional community
- niche market website – Your niche market website should position you as the authority in your industry

Deliver your personal brand identity elements in your:

- email newsletter
- social networking sites
- web portfolio
- profile
- testimonials
- branded biography

One of the best brand themes I have seen is the Wealth Alliance Group. Check out their website, www.wealthalliancegroup.com. All of the programs and training are themed around the movie "*Top Gun*". You have instructors. You are the elite. You have a call sign. My WAG call sign is "Stratagem".

SEO your brand by determining the best branded:

- domain names
- domain theme
- page titles, meta tags, and keywords
- website design
- site map
- interactivity
- email addresses
- email signature files

- email subject lines
- email address lines
- email auto responders
- privacy policy
- spam policy

YOUR PERSONAL DOMAIN

It may seem a bit self-centered, but reinforcing your own name is key to creating a brand name for yourself. Consider your personal domain website or blog, your online CV or resume or portfolio. With increased online reference checking within recruitment processes, establishing your CV online becomes essential. For example, Tom Peters is the co-author of *In Search of Excellence*, a book that changed the world. Tom has a well branded site map which includes:

- Tom Peters
- Tom's latest observations
- Who's Tom
- Where's Tom
- Tom's Ideas
- Tom in the Media
- Tom's Latest Cool Friend

YOUR SIGNATURE CUSTOMER TOUCH POINT

List all of your customer touch points. Are they in your target audiences preferred tone, manner and method?

In addition to thinking about the identity we want to project, we should be asking ourselves, "How do I want to make others feel?" Happy? Enthusiastic? Relieved? Inspired? Safe? How people feel about us is so much more important than what we think about ourselves.

When our personal brand is intentionally able to influence how people feel, we will be able to lead them where we want them to go, as well as drive positive change in the world.

Does that culture reflect in your business, work environment, customer touch points? Your business has customer touch points which all are part of your brand's packaging.

Think of the following as another kind of package and be as attentive to its composition, color, layout, type face as your business card, resume or corporate brochure.

Your Desk and Work Environment
Business image and morale can be improved by upgrading the office and workspaces to appear clean, tidy and professional. This may include new office and reception furniture as well as vehicles that are detailed and restocked.

Your Email Signature
What's your signature sign off? Include a great quote or a testimonial. Definitely include your contact details.

Your Marketing Material
Review your marketing material, website, stationery and promotional material. It may need additional time and resources and should be budgeted accordingly. Is it consistent, branded and in line with your preferred image?

Your Correspondence
Your professional business image must be consistent. Use templates, stationery, scripts and consistent procedures. You are quickly able to do what needs doing, knowing that it will be promoting an effective business image.

Your Client Greetings
Whether it is an answering machine message, a telephone greeting or a response to client queries, consistency in your message or business image is necessary to assure clients that you can deliver, that your promise is the same today as tomorrow.

Your Customer Service Policies

Annually review your client service policies and responses and seek feedback from your staff on what they believe is professional, realistic and appropriate.

An interesting aspect to human behavior is that we will behave consistently with a commitment we have made. This underlines the importance of you and your staff's ownership of outcomes as well as taking the time to commit to designing and then implementing your improved business image.

As a commitment device, a written acceptance to maintain and uphold the business image of the company at all times has great advantages. Research has concluded that whenever one takes a stand that is visible to others, there arises a drive to maintain that stand in order to look like a consistent person.

Your Conduct and Appearance

Look at the leaders in your field and model them. If you look like the top people in your field, you are inevitably on the path to the top. Many companies change their results by establishing a dress code for the people in their company who deal with clients.

They know the importance of appearance. They recognize that people make lasting and important decisions based on how the business looks on the outside. Your business image must reflect your brand. Your brand should identify you as a leader, be distinctive and visible as well as consistent.

Your Attire or Staff Uniforms

Adopt a big business approach. An appropriate dress code is a core part of every business image. Develop a look, which is comfortable, smart and easy to maintain, and make it your unofficial uniform.

Your business "uniform" should reflect the image, values and standards of your business. Determine which universal colors will suit all staff if a uniform approach is adopted. A coordinated, consistent and professional image becomes your signature. You become a professional brand.

When seeking this commitment from staff, provide an explanation of why you are implementing new measures such as staff uniforms or codes of conduct, because people simply like reasons for doing what they do.

Ensure your staff understands how important their image is to you. Timing can be everything. Strategically plan the introduction of various aspects of your new image. Ensure that your staff have sufficient time to buy-in to the changes and that those changes are clearly understood.

Ask yourself some questions.

- Do you dress and look like a first class professional, in every respect, when you go to work, and when you meet with your customers or suppliers?
- Are you proud of the appearance of your staff?
- Do you feel happy to introduce your staff, with the way they currently dress and look on the outside, to your customers and suppliers?
- Are your staff neat, clean, organized and attractive?
- Are you proud to have critical customers visit you and walk around your facilities?

YOUR SIGNATURE RITUAL

Speakers and presenters often have a custom ritual which breaks state and refreshes the energy. What are your personal break state rituals?

You often see presenters or even footballers who score a try display a signature move. What's your custom ritual or gesture?

What's your weekly reward or ritual for being good or achieving good results?

YOUR SIGNATURE THEME SONG

Is there a particular movie or interest you have that aligns to your brand? What's your favorite song? Is it your theme song?

Robert Kiyosaki, author of the *Rich Dad, Poor Dad* series of books, has a theme song. It is Kenny Rogers', *"Gambler"*. It is heard at every one of his live training seminars. I cannot think of the song without thinking of Robert Kiyosaki.

I recently saw a video of the world's best female snowboarders sponsored by Roxy; this video captures their world tour. The song "Walking On Sunshine" obviously was the theme song of this tour. More importantly, the song and the candidate video capture the essence of the Roxy brand. For me, Cher's *Greatest Hits* album literally covers off every aspect of my life, quite nicely.

- What's your life's theme song?
- What's your business theme song?
- What's your favorite sad song?
- What's song lifts up your spirits?
- What's your inspirational song?

List your preferred royalty free intro music:

YOUR BRAND IDENTITY IMPLEMENTATION CHECKLIST

The identity planning process begins, and ends, with a detailed checklist.

At the beginning, you will audit all existing corporate communications, to assess the content, consistency and quality of the currently communicated identity message. It helps to have a checklist of the media to be collected.

At the end of planning, the beginning of the design phase, you will need a checklist of the items which need to be redesigned.

Here is a "typical" corporate identity implementation plan one-page checklist:

- business cards
- fax cover sheet
- forms – e.g. purchase orders
- notepads
- binders
- presentation slide formats
- web sites
- Internet
- intranet
- extranet
- PR / IR communications
- news release
- press kit folder
- HR communications
- recruitment material formats / signatures
- facilities signs
- vehicles
- print ad signature
- electronic presentation formats [PowerPoint etc.]
- broadcast/video signature
- identity guidelines
- graphic standards manual, printed or web-based
- electronic templates
- logo sheets and color chips
- visual "voice" brochure
- identity introduction
- launch brochure
- video
- gifts internal (hats, shirts, ties, pins, etc.)
- gifts external (pens, etc.)

Chapter 13

Action Step 6.
Develop Your Brand's Signature Style

Image ... Impact ... Influence.

The packaging of your brand is a powerful tool that, if used correctly, can influence a customer to buy. Your packaging is not camouflage; rather it is a method of communicating the essential essence of your brand at a glance.

Three in four people (seventy-five percent) said that a person's appearance on the job is likely to affect whether they are taken seriously.

Determine that you want to be the best in your field. Your image is a reflection of what you're capable of. Do you dress and look like a first class professional?

Cultivating a strategic personal style or signature style is what this chapter is all about. You start by identifying your best colors and styles, personality/attitude; you recognize and become comfortable with your personal style markers or statement pieces and then fully integrate them into your personal brand strategic style.

Think strategically when developing a professional image or brand identity to get that job offer, gain that promotion or win that client. Take control of the decisions others are making of you. Your brand can tell your customers about your key attributes through packaging or your strategic style.

Think of what commitment to excellence a professional image says about a person. It indicates discipline, self-respect, focus, class, intelligence, courteousness and good manners.

Creating an impact with your image to leverage your abilities and skyrocket your success is easy when you develop and determine your:

- personal brand presence
- personality style
- strategic identity
- signature style

Your professional image must reflect your brand. Your brand should identify you as a leader and, therefore, should be distinctive and visible as well as consistent.

Your professional image is important because as we've said, sixty-seven percent of first impressions are accurate. There is no second chance. The initial evaluative judgment a person makes about you is very powerful and extremely difficult to change.

Your clients will judge you quickly by your appearance. A decision about your abilities, capabilities and effectiveness are determined initially by what you wear before you say a word.

Adopt a big business approach. An appropriate dress code is a core part of every professional image. Develop a look which is comfortable, smart and easy to maintain, and make it your unofficial uniform. Your brand uniform should reflect the image, values and standards of your business. A coordinated, consistent and professional image becomes your signature. You become a professional brand.

Dress is a powerful and quick way to start building personal brand equity. Expectations create reality. If we look smart, people will give us the benefit of the doubt and think we are clever until we prove them wrong.

What expectation do you create with your dress? Would people expect you to be smart, professional, reliable, trustworthy, disciplined or skilful? That you're a VIP!

BRAND YOURSELF AND DEVELOP YOUR SIGNATURE STYLE

Dressing for success means dressing in a manner that reflects your authentic self in a way that attracts your target audience. Establish a signature style that's memorable.

To determine your best signature style, it is important to initially understand the parameters of your personal brand by developing your personal brand strategic identity and then creating an image or signature style that resonates with your brand. Your brand wants to reassure its audience by the way it looks and at the same time demonstrate some of its best characteristics.

These are the components to creating the right strategic identity for your brand:

- your best personal colors
- your best personal style
- your personality style
- your brand personality and archetype
- your environment

Taking the above components we then create the more appropriate image for your Signature Style. Your signature style or look will include your:

- signature style
- personal presentation
- personal brand style markers

YOUR BEST PERSONAL COLORS

Color makes a difference. Your choice of color will strongly affect the overall impression you make on others. Color has been shown to affect how professional people are judged to be. The colors you wear should be indicative of your level of professionalism, sophistication, and must be appropriate for the occasion. Understanding color contrast and why it is so important is invaluable to your brand.

If you are the business owner, ensure you look your best in your signature brand colors. Invest in a personal color consultation with a professional image consultant to identify your best personal colors. Knowing your best colors and color contrast is vital. You will be seen as more competent, vibrant and healthy in the correct colors.

YOUR BEST PERSONAL STYLE

Style is important. When upgrading your professional image, style includes appearing in a way which reflects your individuality and current trends. Having style sends the message you are confident in yourself and your business.

Style is about projecting an accurate sense of yourself and your business.

Ensure you and your staff identify with the brand image and your unique brand attributes. If you are the business owner or in a senior staff role, invest in a personal style consultation with a professional image consultant to identify the most attractive styles for your body shape, and other programs to assist you develop your own signature style to brand yourself effectively.

See *Additional Resources Available* below for further information on this.

It is important to dress well and understand your best personal colors and styles. The best investment you can make in your wardrobe is an e-Style Portfolio.

For more information go to: www.yourownsignaturestyle.com

YOUR PERSONAL PERSONALITY STYLE

What personality best represents you?

Are you:

1. classic
2. creative
3. dramatic
4. natural or rugged
5. sexy
6. feminine or masculine
7. elegant or sleek

To discover your personal style create a look book. Creating a collage will reveal your brand's packaging preferences. Cut out pictures from fashion magazines that are expressive of your brand and convey a message about your personality and attributes.

Consider how you could adapt it to your business environment. Create a unique, professional fashion statement that you think will be noticed and accepted by your audience.

Remember that there are four important subliminal components to your image and the impressions you make:

1. your credibility
2. your likeability
3. your personal attractiveness
4. your confidence

Your audience is going to be consciously and unconsciously influenced by your appearance. Your image should make you feel powerful, bold and in charge.

YOUR BRAND PERSONALITY AND YOUR BRAND ARCHETYPE

What is your personal brand's personality style? Your brand should embody the word. You can build extraordinary brand power through the use of archetypes in your brand creation and your brand positioning strategy.

Archetypes sometimes have an image or a number of elements which allow them to be easily recognized.

Consider traditional branding archetypes below and in more detail in the previous Chapter.

- maverick (rebel, outlaw, rogue)
- everyman (good old boy, girl next door, average Joe)
- innocent (saint, goody-two-shoes, angel)
- entertainer (clown, jester, performer)
- villain (bad guy, monster, vampire)
- intellectual (sage, genius, expert)
- sensualist (hedonist, pleasure seeker)
- servant (martyr, slave, monk)
- traditionalist (conservative, old school, miser)

Consider the look or image that would be consistent or stereotypically aligned to the archetypes you have chosen for your brand.

YOUR ENVIRONMENT

The most important aspect of dressing professionally is the appropriateness of your dress. It signals that the wearer is aware and understands what level of dress is most suitable for their position, industry, business occasion, figure type, weight, age and the message that they wish to transmit.

Ask yourself these questions:

- What is my industry?
- What is my position?
- What message do I wish to portray?

Word of Warning

Distinguish yourself from your competition and the rest of the crowd, but don't look so out of touch as to give the impression you'd never fit in. Likewise, being too fashion forward can also hinder your brand, as your interest in fashion may be considered greater than your work or your clients.

Within many professional environments there is a silent, but precise standard of dress. If not adhered to, violations of these unwritten codes may result in a stagnant career path, non-engagement or in extreme cases an invitation to look for another place of work.

It is important to discover the appropriate code of dress for each work place, profession or industry even before applying for the position or soliciting work. Attending interviews and functions dressed appropriately will give you a definite advantage. Dress codes ensure that everyone gives the exact image that will solicit the most work and imply greatest confidence in their level and field of expertise.

Make the right decision about your appearance each day.

Consider the following:

- the day's agenda
- job/position – corporate image
- interaction with: colleagues, team members, clients or consultants
- daily responsibilities
- agenda – objective
- audience – client expectation
- activities

- responsibilities for the day
  - meetings: audience
  - colleagues: how they dress
  - supervisor: how he/she dresses
  - clients: new or existing, how they dress, their industry/profession
  - location: in or out of the office, town or county
- desired perception and preferred image
  - powerful/authoritative
  - credible/respectful
  - professional/efficient
  - knowledgeable/friendly
  - accessible/friendly
  - creative/original

While not all work places expect you to wear a suit to work, it will make you most comfortable when you understand what level of dress you are expected to wear.

A fact, which has been confirmed by many studies, is that individuals who have a professional image, are appropriately attired and/or have the trappings of authority, are accorded more attention or obedience by those they encounter.

Improving your professional image increases your persuasiveness and mobility. Take advantage of this principle.

An effective professional image should reflect these qualities, as outlined previously the should be:

- credible
- congruent
- attractive
- appropriate
- confident
- consistent
- of a positive stereotype

YOUR SIGNATURE STYLE

Creating a Signature Style is an investment in building your personal brand and leveraging your professional profile.

These are style essentials for every brand:

- spend money on one good black suit
- always tailor your clothes to fit
- ensure shoes are in good repair and polished
- buy high quality, more classic and conservative styles
- stay contemporary with a new pair of glasses every year if you wear them
- update your hair every year and ladies likewise your makeup
- find a signature piece or develop a signature look
- look for role models in your industry ...
  what are the best wearing
- outwardly express your brand's attributes
- consciously consider your audience's preferences

> A celebrity is more influential when they have a definable style.
> — Rachel Quilty

To impressively brand yourself you must have a Style. In a recent interview with the Today show, Jump the Q® highlighted the benefits of developing a signature style, particularly if you are a busy professional.

Create a Signature Style by considering the following:

- Decide your favorite item, statement piece or style marker which makes you look and feel great and which is consistent with your brand identity.
- Create several looks using that one item. You may want to start a scrapbook or look book of magazine pictures you like.
- Make sure the look suits your style personality, whether it is classic, dramatic, elegant ... so you feel comfortable.
- Select a look that suits your body shape and personal coloring.
- Create a look that is easy to clean, maintain and is practical.

There are many benefits to branding yourself with a signature style. The advantages are huge. This almost "uniform" approach enables you be out the door quickly. Benefits include:

- you can buy multiples of the same item
- you can easily coordinate items and accessories
- with only a few pieces you can create several looks
- with a coordinated look you never get caught looking like you just grabbed anything
- its good psychology – when you look good, with a signature style, you feel good
- a uniform approach creates order and you can more efficiently get out the door

When upgrading your image, style is important. Style includes appearing good in a way that reflects your individuality and current trends. Having style sends the message that you are confident in yourself and your business.

Style is about projecting an accurate sense of yourself and your business. So, it's important to ensure you and your staff identify with the business image and your unique business elements.

We wear twenty percent of our wardrobe eighty percent of the time. Eighty percent of our wardrobe just sits. That's an expensive waste. Most wardrobes contain five hundred to five thousand dollars worth of clothes never or rarely worn.

Thirteen items can be combined into over a hundred different outfits. You can dress well on any budget. Do yourself a favor and purchase good quality basics and update with new season trend pieces. The basic rule is ... buy fewer pieces in a better quality.

YOUR PERSONAL PRESENTATION

Important tips on personal presentation:

- Always be well groomed, neat and tidy and apply attention to appropriate personal hygiene.
- Always ensure your shoes are shined at all times and your fingernails are clean and neat.
- After coffee have a mint, use deodorant throughout the day as needed, and consider cleaning your teeth after eating as well.
- Do a regular mirror check, tidiness, well maintained makeup, five o'clock shadow, and teeth.
- Update your hair style annually, likewise ladies your make up.

Psychology plays an important role in image management and how you are perceived. If a person has poor hygiene, or is overweight, often unkind judgments are made about this person's quality of work and their work ethic. Don't sabotage your career and success by not looking after yourself and neglecting your health and grooming.

Social psychology studies have discovered that when you make a change and also change your physical appearance, you are sixty percent more likely to change permanently. In the process of change, when we change the physical, we are more likely to change the mental, as well as the spiritual.

Updating your image can give you a significant psychological lift.

Let's now consider your personal touch points and what message they convey about your personal brand:

- your hairstyle
- your personal grooming
- your make-up
- your jewelry
- your hygiene

- your clothing
- your shoes, tie and belt
- your briefcase and/or hand bag
- your business card
- your work satchel/briefcase

YOUR PERSONAL BRAND STYLE MARKERS

Your key personal brand style markers are also part of your brand positioning strategy.

Ensure your personal brand commands authority. Whether it is a uniform, vehicle or stationery; the trappings of power or wealth should be consistent with your position as an expert in your field as people are easily swayed by the appearance of authority.

There are other aspects of your packaging that are worth a thousand words.

Your brand accessories should speak in your voice and communicate something about you and what your values are. Be on notice. Everything we say and do impacts our personal brand equity:

- how we dress
- how we articulate our message
- how we listen
- how we follow through
- who our friends are

Everything says something about you. We have mentioned customer touch points in a business sense.

Become comfortable with your personal style markers, statement pieces and signature style then fully integrate them into your brand strategy. Your brand can tell your customers about your key attributes through packaging.

Let's focus on a few which may be playing a vital role in the message you communicate about your brand and to determine whether it is an accurate reflection of you.

- your car
- your watch
- your resume
- your promotional portfolio
- your photo book
- your brand packaging
- your personal presence
- your first impression
- your introduction
- your presenting skills
- your vocal style
- your telephone manner
- your elevator speech
- your confidence
- your signature uniform
- your signature gift
- your behavior
- your purchases and donations
- your manners

YOUR CAR

People notice what type of car you drive. Look for a model and color that reflects your brand and personality. Always make sure your car is immaculate.

YOUR WATCH

Investing in a quality time piece tells others a lot about you. Your time is important. You pay attention and monitor time and have a degree of attention to detail.

YOUR RESUME

Whether it's multimedia or traditional ... ensure it is the best quality you can afford and appropriate for your audience. It makes a statement about your work ethic and interest in your job. It's all part of your brand campaign. Inject some zing with your greatest attributes.

You want your brand's core values and your unique expertise to shine through your resume. Include your personal mission statement and outline your brand's best qualities in the covering letter. Make your writing personable. Hire someone to help you, if necessary. It is as important as your interview outfit.

YOUR PROMOTIONAL PORTFOLIO

Proudly present your work in a great leather binder, a multimedia DVD, an interesting box, an artistic case or some other method that reflects your brand. When sending out your promotional material, send it with something reflecting your brand, in an unusual box, with a gift that sets you apart.

YOUR PHOTO BOOK

Let your images sell for you (a touch more on the power of photos). Put photo books to work for your business. A photo book is an actual hard or soft covered book you make yourself from your photos. You select the combination of pictures, the orientation, the layout, text to write with them. They vary from fourteen to twenty pages and different sizes. They're relatively inexpensive and quick – if not immediate to do.

YOUR BRAND PACKAGING

Is there a manner in which you can introduce your corporate colors into your wardrobe? What colors are worn in your business environment and industry? What colors reflect your specific brand culture?

YOUR PERSONAL PRESENCE

Often when we consider style we stop at the outer packaging. Your presentation is just as important as your packaging. Presentation is your tone, communications style, mannerisms, performance and attitude. This is your unique "voice" and gives authority and authenticity to your personal brand.

How do you communicate your personality? What's your style? Think of your key attributes – how do you show them? Do your values reflect in what you do and say? When you are congruent and comfortable in your skin that's when your true self is revealed.

YOUR FIRST IMPRESSION

First impressions count. Often it's less about what we say than how we actually say it.

The impact of visibility and tonality dramatically increases when conducting a presentation or speech. Therefore the emotional impact of the presentation is greatly amplified through our appearance and attitude.

How do you present yourself? Are you confident and tall? Do you fidget? Do you carry yourself with pride? Does your image instill you with confidence, make you feel powerful, bold and in charge?

YOUR INTRODUCTION

Your introduction and entrance style should project a long term, going somewhere brand that is all about success. One of the best methods for improvement is to carry yourself like a CEO.

- Walk in like you own the place. Don't hesitate.
- Walk and stand tall. Height adds authority.
- Walk proudly. A striding manner is perceived as confident and credible.
- Be passionate. Use positive, powerful physical communicators – wide eyes, gentle nod, leaning forward.
- Be attractive and engaging. Beauty can be daunting so be friendly and engaging to capture your audience.

Your aim should be to tell people who you are and give them a pleasant experience of you.

YOUR HANDSHAKE

Never underestimate the importance of your hand shake. Given the amount of science and study attributed to this gesture, it would be wise to develop a firm and confident hand shake.

Work is a professional arena where your behavior can make or break your career. No kissing at work functions is a good rule of thumb. A firm handshake, warm greeting, good eye contact and a smile will express your professionalism quietly and effectively.

A friendly handshake signals that you are aware and understand what level of conduct is most suitable for the occasion and conveys the message you wish to transmit on initial acquaintance, that you are someone who comes to work, to work.

Always aim to look and behave like a professional and you'll be treated like one.

YOUR PRESENTING SKILLS

Learning to communicate successful is a valuable tool for success. Present yourself with intelligence, charm and sophistication when you communicate. Excellence in communication is one of the most desirable qualities your brand could possess.

The more people you are able to inform and touch, the more powerful your brand. Always say yes to the opportunity to present.

Use small meeting formats and group gatherings to practice your presentation skills. Preparation and rehearsal are the best methods of overcoming fear of public speaking. The trick to a great presentation is to make a connection with your listeners.

YOUR VOCAL STYLE

Over twenty percent of a speech's effectiveness relates to tonality, pitch and pace. Identify if you have any unusual or distracting vocal qualities – loud laugh, broad accent, uncommon speak patterns. Speech and vocal coaching may be an excellent investment in your brand. Literally all celebrities have at one point received coaching on voice and presentation.

Proper pronunciation can assist your listeners to connect. Developing voice confidence instills confidence in your audience. Learning to modulate your voice makes everything you say more interesting. Lowering your voice can add authority. Small adjustments in your voice production can have a dramatic effect on your presentation.

YOUR TELEPHONE MANNER

When on the telephone your voice is even more important than when you are having a conversation. You may wish to record yourself reading. When you listen to yourself identify any areas of improvement.

Being conversational is also important. Your ability to tell a story without hesitation and unusual vocal patterns will be a great asset in generating rapport. Speak with a smile. You may also wish to stand as this adds authority to your conversational tone.

YOUR ELEVATOR SPEECH

The ability to think on your feet and express yourself succinctly and successfully will greatly increase your brand equity. How easy you are able to speak on your feet depends greatly on your confidence and your inner knowledge that you can do it.

YOUR CONFIDENCE

Every successful brand must be able to confidently communicate in public. You must put your brand in front of people and that requires you to speak in front of people.

YOUR SIGNATURE UNIFORM

Why adopt a "uniform" approach? Necessity! Your professional image must be consistent. Just like using templates, stationery, scripts, systems and consistent procedures, developing a uniform approach to dressing impacts on your psychology.

You will be more productive and more efficient. You are quickly able to do what is required, knowing it will promote an effective business image.

YOUR SIGNATURE GIFT

Small, unexpected, classy gestures separate us from our competitors and make an impact. Little gestures have significant impact. It becomes very apparent to the receiver the level of thought or care that goes into your gift ... so consider it carefully to make the right impression.

YOUR BEHAVIOR

People expect great service, but they don't necessarily expect to receive a caring gesture or gift. Exceptional response times or a thorough follow up shortly after an initial meeting cements your brand and ensures you remain memorable. People will begin to emulate you. This is personal branding in motion.

YOUR PURCHASES AND DONATIONS

As a consumer, you are also personally branded by the various corporate brands you support. We see Victoria Beckham purchasing only Hermes handbags; the Olsen twins are inseparable from their Starbuck's purchases. There are endless charities that we see celebrities support and align their brand to.

What purchases and donations do you make and how do they reflect on your brand?

YOUR MANNERS

The ability to get along with others, demonstrates good manners. Perform acts of consideration and put others at ease. While these qualities have always been appreciated, in today's hectic and often self-centered world they act as beacons that cause a person to shine out from the crowd.

True acts of courtesy are performed, not out of a sense of obligation or in a patronizing way, but out of genuine respect, care and thoughtfulness for the person(s) in question, regardless of any cultural, political or religious differences. Of course, etiquette for etiquette's sake will be an empty and meaningless activity, but genuine good manners and a working knowledge of professional behavior are essential and productive business skills.

Other issues which may be adding or detracting from your brand include:

- our immediate friends
- your reading habits
- your routine
- your jokes
- your language

In the end, to have a great personal brand you have to develop your own style in support of your brand, first know your personality – those visible, audible, behavioral aspects of your character. Style is about your personal presence.

When planned, your personal brand identity allows you to tell your audience what you want to say about yourself and how you want to be perceived. A good personal brand identity will visually separate and distinguish you and your products and services from all others.

Chapter 14

Action Step 7.
Devise Your Personal Brand Marketing Plan

One key to succeeding in the market place is to have your message out there; if not continuously, then often enough to keep your name alive in customers minds. This is the meaning of visibility and if you're not visible to your potential clients, you cease to exist.

By now you should have a clear understanding of who your target market is.
You should be easily able to answer these questions:

- Who is your target audience?
- Who do you want to impress and do business with?

This chapter will assist you to market, package and promote yourself to achieve your personal brand goals.

The "How" part of your personal brand should be a solid marketing plan and a strategic communication plan, dealt with in a later Action Step. This is the platform from which you'll launch your personal brand goals. Specifically within this chapter we will look at:

- your marketing mix
- your marketing plan
- your marketing strategies
- your "go to market" strategy
- your brand positioning

It is essential to develop a personal brand marketing plan to build and maintain your brand name awareness, now that we have designed your brand identity and style.

Any marketing you do to promote your brand should strive to accomplish the following:

- communicate your promise and mission
- highlight your key attributes
- reinforce your message
- efficiently and effectively reach your target audience
- make a positive impact and invite action

Wikipedia® defines marketing as the process by which companies create customer interest in products or services. It generates the strategy that underlies sales techniques, business communication, and business development. It is an integrated process through which companies build strong customer relationships and create value for their customers and for themselves.

Marketing is used to identify the customer, to satisfy the customer, and to keep the customer. With the customer as the focus of its activities, the adoption of marketing strategies requires businesses to shift their attention from production to the perceived needs and wants of their customers as the means of staying profitable.

Research has shown time and again there is a direct correlation between a product's level of awareness and its market share. The greater the brand name awareness the greater the market share. This is why large organizations spend a lot of money within the advertising component of their marketing budgets. An important point to note is that these same organizations spend considerable energy on ensuring they use the right marketing channels to target their ideal customer. Small business often overlooks this critical stage and wastes money on ineffective advertising campaigns.

In order to create perceptions, a steady flow of information is needed to raise awareness. Remember your goal is to control the flow of information about you, and to do that you must provide information that clearly defines your business, which in turn is you!

Even more fascinating is the fairly common perception that a better known product is a better product; whether it is or not.

> The aim of marketing is to know and understand the customer so well the product or service fits and sells itself.　— *Peter Drucker*

Your Marketing Mix

The Market Plan outlines your game plan to achieve your marketing objectives and should include information about the 4Ps of marketing: product, price, place and promotion. Consider a slight variation on the 4P's Marketing Mix, known more formally as an Offer Definition:

1. Product definition: You are the product!
   - What are you selling?
   - What are you offering to the marketplace?
2. Price – How much will you charge for it?
3. Place –
   - How will your customers acquire your offering?
   - How will they hear about your personal brand?
4. Promotion – How will customers learn about you?

Plus the two personal branding essential Ps:

5. Positioning
   - How will you be positioned in your customer's minds?
   - What's your niche?
6. Packaging – How will the product or service look?

The key to getting your marketing mix right is to understand your customers, know your competition, be aware of your market, review your offering on a regular basis and get your business known and trusted by customers and potential customers in your target market.

YOUR PERSONAL BRAND MARKETING PLAN

A Personal Brand Marketing Plan is defined as a written document that describes your advertising and marketing efforts generally for the coming year; it includes a statement of the marketing situation, a discussion of target markets and your personal brand positioning, and a description of the marketing mix you intend to use to reach your marketing goals.

Create a five-part marketing plan for your personal brand:

Part 1: Situational Analysis

This introductory section contains an overview of your situation as it exists today and will provide a useful benchmark as you adapt and refine your plan in the coming months. Begin by undertaking a Situational Analysis with a short description of your current product or service offering, then a SWOTT analysis of the marketing advantages and challenges you face, and a look at the threats posed by your competitors.

Describe any outside forces that will affect your business in the coming year such as marketplace trends.

Part 2: Target Audience

All that's needed here is a simple, bulleted description of your target audiences. If you're marketing to consumers, write a target-audience profile based on demographics, including age, gender and any other important characteristics. Business to Business marketers should list your target audiences by category (such as lawyers, doctors, shopping malls) and include any qualifying criteria for each.

Part 3: Goals

In one page or less, list your personal brand's marketing goals for the coming year. The key is to make your goals realistic and measurable so that you can easily evaluate your performance.

Part 4: Strategies and Tactics

Develop your marketing strategies for achieving your marketing goals and list each of the corresponding tactics you'll employ to execute them.

Your tactics section should include all the actionable steps you plan to take for advertising, public relations, direct mail, trade shows and special promotions. You can use a calendar to schedule your tactics or use a contact manager or spreadsheet program. Stick to your schedule and follow through.

Part 5: Budget

The final section of your plan includes a brief breakdown of the costs associated with each of your tactics. So if you plan to exhibit at three trade shows per year, for example, you'll include the costs to participate in the shows and prepare your booth and marketing materials. If you find the tactics you've selected are too costly, you can go back and make revisions before you arrive at a final budget.

You can adapt this plan as your business grows and your marketing programs evolve.

YOUR MARKETING STRATEGIES

Selecting the right conduits for getting your message to your target market and building brand awareness is essential.

Marketing consists of three basic strategies – publicity, advertising, and promotion. Within this chapter we look at the various avenues you can select to promote and market your brand.

PUBLICITY

Generating free publicity is actually easier than you think. And once you start the process can quickly snow ball into numerous unsolicited opportunities. The opportunities come to you rather than you chasing them.

Even as a new brand in a competitive marketplace you can discover and maximize plenty of free publicity and public relations opportunities to let people know you exist.

Editorial coverage has the added power of being more credible than paid advertising and carries an unbiased stamp of approval that advertising doesn't.

Publicize everything your brand accomplishes. The objective of publicizing your brand is to create visibility and strong word of mouth coverage.

Tackle publicity with this simple three step process:

1. Identify the media channels you'd like to target. Is there a magazine, TV program or blog that your target market is more likely to tune into?

2. Identify the journalists, executive producers or editors of these mediums, obtain their details and educate yourself on their style and story angles.

3. Develop a relationship by email or telephone, always respectful of their time. Consistently pitch and distribute newsworthy content. The story may relate to your business or a client.

Regardless of the outcome, request some feedback on their preferences. Keep in close contact with your industry, build your visibility within your target market and build a profile within your community. Often a story has more than one interviewee and if you are well known within your industry, you may be recommended as a possible guest. Opportunities may present themselves from a possible competitor.

Follow up any requests from journalists. Put together a Press Kit to distribute to the media. This may contain a bio, head shot, show-reel, sample interview questions.

> A good advertisement is one which sells the product without drawing attention to itself."   — David Ogilvy

Advertising is generally considered to be any activity attracting public attention to a product or business, via a paid announcement in the print, broadcast, or electronic media.

Advertising is often considered costly. However, advertising can be very inexpensive. When you write a newsletter you are advertising. If you post a blog you may be advertising your goods and services. Every advertisement should be thought of as a contribution to your personal brand.

Consider these methods of obtaining free advertising:

- website
- mail campaign
- niche market blog
- personal blog
- networking and word of mouth

AUTHORITATIVE COMPANY WEBSITE

When properly set up and maintained, a website becomes a virtual brand office and around the clock salesperson for your business.

As a resource for your industry, your website can feature lots of useful information, including articles, links, downloadable files, and customer resources. It is also one of the most effective channels for establishing strategic alliances, facilitating co-promotions, promoting online classes and seminars and reaching a global audience.

EMAIL NEWSLETTER

To make the most of your business relations, you need to keep in touch regularly with everyone who's part of your business world – your clients, customers, vendors, associates, and prospects. Newsletters are an excellent way to keep in touch with all of them, and maintain their awareness of your brand. A newsletter can help you increase customer loyalty, and make those who've never met you feel like they've known you for years.

Email newsletters can be used to:

- distribute articles, tip sheets, and anything else you've written
- express your opinion about topics related to your business
- direct recipients to your web site, helping you sell more products and services

- help the media and other centers of influence stay attuned to your business
- increase income by selling products and services through affiliate arrangements
- encourage feedback from clients and customers

Here are some things we do to build relationships:

- weekly special news updates
- special emails and broadcasts on news, free information, etc
- free webinars to review our course material and get our students engaged
- blog posts on all of our sites
- private emails and phone calls

Other channels include:

- niche market blog
- personal brand blog

Just a small note on networking; your personal brand will benefit from having a well-nurtured professional network. Be accessible. Develop plans to build and maintain yours. Remember your network extends your brand for you with strong brand ambassadors.

An important distinction is that you don't just network, you niche network. Ensure you meet "centers of influence". If you gain their trust, they can spread the word about you within their network and give you credibility.

Networking also provides excellent strategic alliance opportunities. Joint ventures or strategic alliances provide one of the least expensive, most efficient, least time consuming, most consuming, most credible methods for marketing a business; and provide a way to reach larger audiences for less money by pooling resources. Creativity makes the possibilities for cross promotions infinite.

TRADITIONAL ADVERTISING

Don't overlooking the importance of traditional advertising if it is appropriate in your arena. Monitor and measure your results. It makes sense to focus and invest in areas impacting on your client's perception of you and your business. Updating or re-positioning your business brand can be effective in capturing a greater market, building presence and ensuring long term business success.

Paid advertising may include:

- newspapers
- magazines
- cable TV
- broadcast TV
- radio
- Internet
- billboards
- bus, train/subway, city bench
- merchandise with your logo
- Google Adwords (pay per click or PPC)
- online advertisements

People routinely ignore anything that resembles advertising. The challenge is to make the experience of your brand warm and inviting – to create the feeling that a real human is on the other end of that interaction. That's why creating an honest and personal connection with people is so crucial.

PROMOTION

Promotions can also enhance your brand's desirability. When you set out to develop a promotion for your brand make sure that it gets you noticed in the right way. Each promotion that you execute on behalf of your personal brand should meet the following objectives:

- generate brand awareness and build brand equity
- reflect your brand's core values
- reinforce your position

Promotions may include competitions, tie-ins, value added gifts and special events.

YOUR "GO TO MARKET" STRATEGY

Your marketing goals, sometimes called objectives, are measurable milestones that lead you to your business goal. Each goal should lead to sales otherwise you should define it differently. Remember your goals should be S.M.A.R.T.

S = Specific about what you want to achieve
M = Measurable so you can track your progress
A = Achievable
R = Relevant to the target market you wish to influence
T = Time-based, usually a short period of time (no more than a year)

Some simple examples:

1. increase existing customer base by twenty-five percent by end of year
2. to increase repeat business within your client base by thirty percent this year
3. to achieve twenty percent of your revenue by offering new affordable services
4. to attract five new customers per month from xyz segment.

Using the marketing objective stated above (to increase repeat business within your client base by thirty percent this year); you might develop a marketing strategy such as create promotional materials e.g., an e-Newsletter and a complimentary seminar series that includes knowledge and valuable offers to your current clients.

To increase sales using goals, objectives and strategies, each plays a different but interrelated and important role in the success of your business. To develop a successful marketing plan, focus on your marketing objectives and the accompanying strategies. Simply define what you are trying to achieve in measurable, specific terms and how you plan to achieve them in descriptive terms.

Once you have your objectives and strategies, move on to your positioning, messages, and brand. As you continue to develop each layer of your marketing foundation, you will see your marketing effort become more focused, targeted, and consistent – the three ingredients for success.

With any marketing strategy it is important to plan, execute, track and measure its performance.

YOUR BRAND POSITIONING

There are a thousand methods to market your personal brand. Following is an overview of the most successful methods of generating significant publicity and promotional opportunities as well as positioning your brand as the authority within your marketplace. See the Brand Yourself Resources section for additional information.

BECOME A KEYNOTE SPEAKER

Public speaking is an ideal way to build your profile because it showcases your knowledge in a polished form to people who are interested in hearing it. A person who takes the podium is seen as someone who has something worth saying that audience members would like to know themselves.

Speaking can be the fastest, easiest and cheapest way to establish yourself as an expert and it gives you tremendous credibility over time.

Most common speaking opportunities arise at:

- associations
- chambers of commerce
- leads clubs
- continuing education programs
- webinar presentations
- teleconference events

Dr Joanna Martin of Shift Speaker Training advises there are "two angles of marketing that speaking is great for:

1.   branding
2.   attracting new prospects

Nothing positions you more perfectly than stepping onto a stage and speaking.

It makes you the instant expert. Become a speaker so that you can quickly position your personal brand as the authority.

BECOME AN AUTHOR

Darren Stephens is a bestselling author, publisher and a former business partner of John Gray, author of *Men are From Mars, Women are From Venus*. This book alone has gone on to sell over forty million copies, been translated into fifty-four languages, and sold in a hundred and forty-nine countries. It spent six and a half years on the New York Times best seller list between 1992 and 1998, and catapulted John Gray to fame and fortune.

Darren Stephens promotes that, *"Having a best seller is an awesome way to position yourself as THE expert in your niche. Since I helped John Gray become the 'relationships' guru with 'Men Are From Mars, Women are From Venus', he's gone on to build a billion-dollar business"*.

As you can imagine, having a best seller in the major bookstores is a fantastic way to become the recognized expert and to dominate your niche.

BECOME A COLUMNIST

Placing articles in appropriate consumer, business and trade publications is one of the most powerful marketing techniques available. The key to placing articles is to package your ideas as news rather than sales pieces.

Possible publications include:

- professional publications
- trade publications
- newsletters
- local consumer magazines
- websites

Once you have a list of preferred publications, contact the editors. A good query to the editor should contain a strong lead or opening that grabs attention, followed by content that supports and elaborates on the opening and ends with pertinent information on the author and why he/she is qualified to write the article. When producing an article you will need to consider the length, slant and deadline which can be confirmed by the editor.

Always ask if you can use your own bi-line and with a short bio. Both are important parts of your article and are why you are writing for free in the first place. If done properly, your bi-line will encourage a reader response. They can contact you, attend your event, buy your book, request more information etc. Include as much information as possible such as web address, email, description of books, free gifts and offers, add a persuasive description of you and your business.

While you might from time to time contribute editorial content to various publications, becoming a regular columnist clearly establishes your leadership within your marketplace.

BECOME AN ONLINE MEDIA EXPERT

Establishing and building your personal brand can be leveraged when you create an online product presence. Andrew and Daryl Grant of *Our Internet Secrets* have generated a dynamic brand with strong development of online products using e-Books, Clickbank and membership-site products. They advise that the keys to internet success they've found in implementing new online products and projects include:

1. set a clear specific goal
2. prioritize the possible methods you could use to achieve the goal – choose one project to start on
3. prepare a project plan with allocated time and resources – based on a proven home business system
4. follow the plan to completion, monitoring and fine tuning on the way
5. celebrate your success

Andrew and Daryl Grant provide a solution to a new entrant market. By providing solutions for people very new to internet marketing and assisting them to start with a simple online product such as an e-Book, they have become recognized experts in the specific online product niches of e-Book development as well as membership site development.

BECOME A MEDIA PERSONALITY

When you read about a business in the newspaper or in a magazine or hear about it on the radio, chances are you immediately elevate that business above its competitors. It has solidity and credibility.

This is why PR or Public Relations is the ultimate marketing strategy. No other marketing method delivers so much impact for so little investment of time and money. PR is the only form of marketing that produces both public awareness and the implied endorsement that comes with appearing in the media as a news story.

PR generates talk about you. It's an independent validation of your worth. PR is the art of getting the media to give you free coverage.

To get media interested in your business, you have to see the value of your expertise, or tell a story that makes readers interested. Stand back from your business and determine what makes you unique. It's a matter of determining what's distinctive about what you do or what you know, and approaching the media with a carefully crafted pitch or introduction.

Attracting media attention is easy when you become the person journalist's call when they need an industry expert to help them complete their stories. Follow these steps to build your media profile:

- build a media file
- build a list of newspapers, magazines, newsletters, and radio and television programs where you want to get coverage
- build media appeal
- use your distinction to your advantage to attract the media, which is always in search of stories with built in media appeal
- position yourself as an expert resource. Journalists rely on good quotes from experts to make their stories lively, interesting and to lend authority to their discussion. Let the media know that you are available as an authority on a particular subject by introducing yourself to reporters that cover your industry
- pitch your story/stories

There are a number of ways a small business can get coverage:

- alert the media to story ideas within your industry
- position yourself as an industry expert or commentator
- organize and promote a public event
- tie your business to current issues and breaking news
- write articles for trade publications
- showcase an unusual aspect of your business

Create a media plan. Build media appeal and attract media attention. Position yourself as an expert resource.

BECOME A TELEVISION AND RADIO CELEBRITY

Radio and television provide great ways to reach large audiences. By representing yourself as an interesting guest or accessible expert, you'll add authority and insight to their news stories and gain valuable exposure, while helping stations satisfy their endless need to fill airtime.

The broadcast media reaches the ears and eyes of your target market, delivering these powerful benefits:

- greater reach into your marketplace
- a more personal audience connection
- celebrity status of appearing "on the air"
- increased sales

Television and radio rely on interesting guests or accessible experts. You'll add authority and insight to their news stories. And they are always looking for businesses and products that offer some novelty or special angle that will grab their audience's attention.

Appearing on TV or in a video can create an enormous boost to your personal brand. However, appearing before the media can strike fear into the heart of even seasoned veterans. Look or act less than your best, and you may find opinions and opportunities changing direction in less time than it takes to call "you're on".

Once in front of the camera, your visual appearance, attitude and words will combine to create your public image. As a member of a team your actions reflect back on everyone so it makes sense to take time before an interview to consider how to best present yourself.

A media or video interview is your opportunity to enthusiastically, knowledgeably, and succinctly communicate your message and reach your target audience.

Imagine, you are about to be interviewed. You haven't said a word. Yet in those few opening seconds you have made a lasting impression. Your leading attribute in a TV Interview is your personal appearance.

Your appearance plays a substantial role in promoting your personal brand. However, the reporter is relying on you as an expert and you need to be prepared. Smooth and confident delivery of your interview will consolidate your professional image and boost your brand.

It is important to focus on the key message that you wish to deliver. And have prepared three points you wish to make supporting your key message. For example, in a recent interview with the Channel 9 Today show, Jump the Q® focused their message on the benefits of developing a signature style, highlighting three key points for creating a signature style. Firstly, that it was affordable, secondly it saves you time deciding what to wear and lastly, you can co-ordinate your new look effortlessly.

BECOME AN ONLINE WEB CELEBRITY

Your online presence can weaken or strengthen your personal brand. Debra Thompson Roedl, CEO and Marketing Strategist from the Wealth Alliance Group, promotes systematically building your online expert empire. This allows you to support your marketing funnel and address your customer's varying price point preferences. While developing customized and well branded websites, marketing expertise is foundational in the planning stages to ensure that your online brand presence is conveying a consistent and compelling brand message throughout your online expert empire.

The Wealth Alliance team has assisted many of the biggest trainers and speakers in the world develop an online expert empire. Debra recommends, "simultaneously developing your authority site such as a niche specific personal blog and your niche market single product site to establish your expertise quickly."

BECOME A MARKETPLACE PLATFORM SPECIALIST

Your marketplace is no longer limited by who you can attract to walk through your shop door. Platforms such as Google, Amazon, Clickbank, Yahoo and eBay have created enormous online opportunities to building your brand and promote your goods and services.

Matt and Amanda Clarkson developed a program to teach people how to use eBay to create an online business. Matt and Amanda are now recognized as world leaders in eBay education.

They share this advice below, which highlights the need also to connect with the right marketing channel for your target audience.

Step 1. Have a dream big enough that you would do anything to achieve it

Step 2. Choose the right vehicle that will get you there the fastest and most painless way possible

Step 3. Choose mentors who have results you want and follow their proven systems

Amanda adds, *"It is super easy to get started on eBay because you don't have to find the traffic and you don't have to build a website ... eBay does this for you"*.

By educating yourself about a platform not only can you increase your online presence, you can potentially become an expert on that platform and add that to your service offerings.

Note: to leverage some of these platforms it is essential to have a corporation within the United States. If it is necessary to establish your business there Nevada Corporate Planners offer turnkey solutions in building business foundations in the U.S. – business with serviced offices in Las Vegas, a Corporation or legal entity, Employer Tax File number and U.S. Bank account. Extend your business and personal brand into the enormous U.S. market.

This service is the ultimate in leveraging your time and resources. CEO Scott Letourneau is recognized all over the world due to his own successful personal brand, and adds this comment on branding yourself ... *"Let's face it, the economy worldwide has changed dramatically over the last couple of years. If you are serious about being a business success, you must improve your brand and image, it is a key component for survival and growth."*

BECOME THE RESOURCE CENTER FOR YOUR INDUSTRY

Image Innovators.com has become a global resource for Professional Image Consultants. Recognizing that Image Consultants were in need of up-to-date resources and high quality training courses, Image Innovators created resources that image consultants would be proud to use and training courses that were internationally recognized and certified. Ann Reinten, Director of Image Innovators.com gives this advice, *"To become a resource center for your industry, look for ways to improve the resources that are presently being used and to extend their reach. Anyone can now go online and share in a world-wide marketplace if they have a great product and some social and marketing savvy"*.

Ann also offers these three tips to ensure you become a expert resource within your industry:

1. Gain industry certification – many professions have industry associations from which they can gain education and certification. Certification shows industry members and the public that you have reached a professional standard. This is invaluable in creating a brand that has credibility.
2.   Get known for your expertise – contribute into your association and work towards becoming a recognized industry expert.
3. Never stop improving. Revamp and renew products, presentations and all materials regularly to ensure they are up-to-date and relevant.

BECOME THE HUB OF INFORMATION AND RESOURCES FOR YOUR INDUSTRY.

Turn your knowledge into information products that are available at various price points. This allows you to serve all those potential customers who can't afford your personal consulting fee and those who do not live locally.

You can expand your market because your information products provide a range of options at different price points. The results are that your business has something for everyone and converts many smaller prospects into paying customers. Entrepreneurs market and sell information products based on what they know.

So, create online products, webinar series', CDs, DVDs, podcasts, books and e-Books to establish your expertise, reach larger markets and create new income streams.

BECOME A SOCIAL MEDIA GURU

Develop a Social Media Plan. Social media is content that has been created by its own audience. Examples of social media are Facebook®, Twitter®, YouTube®. When someone uses social media successfully they don't just create content; they create conversations. And those conversations create communities. In turn this creates brand loyalty and commitment.

Let's look at Twitter just briefly.

You can build a loyal customer following, expand your brand and generate instant buzz when you integrate Twitter into your existing marketing strategies. The best businesses today and tomorrow are using this high tech, low cost and low hassle technology to gain real advantages over their competitors.

In Joel Comm's book *Twitter Power* he cites that, *"Twitter's largest age demographic is now 35-44 year olds. Forteen percent are stable career types, i.e., young single professionals living in big city metros. Twelve percent are young cosmopolitans – forty-somethings with household income over $250,000 per year."*

Comm provides the following tips for building your brand on Twitter®:

- create an inviting Twitter profile
- choose a brand appropriate picture
- design your Twitter profile to position your brand

OTHER RESOURCES

Additional resources are available at:
www.BrandYourselfforSuccess.com

as well as:
www.learnhowtobrandyourself.com.

These resources provide a practical toolbox of strategies that show you how to:

- get consistent media attention
- use speaking engagements to cultivate your target market
- become a center of influence within your industry
- leverage the internet to its full potential
- create ancillary information products that supplement your income and build public awareness

Chapter 15

Action Step 8.
Decide Your Desired Outcomes
Resources and Skill Set

YOUR PERSONAL BRAND RESOURCE PLAN

Strategic brand planning will be the keystone to your brand's success. And planning your resource requirements is a very valuable and often overlooked component of personal brand planning.

Consider yourself a commander.

- Decide that you are in charge of your very own command center
- Decide what your goal is for your personal brand Make it a self-fulfilling prophecy
- What is your Command Center's objective
- What does it wish to achieve
- What resources are required to achieve these results

This chapter investigates your personal brand goals, their resource requirements and the skill set requirements you will need to achieve them. While this chapter doesn't set out a formal recourse plan, your key objective is to recognize the importance of adequately resourcing your personal brand strategic plan and discovering what may be more achievable than you think.

Another important part of any brand strategic plan consists of analyzing your risk factors and what happens if you don't succeed in relation to your responsibilities. In this we address the "what if" scenarios as outlined in our Momentum Formulae for Success on the following pages.

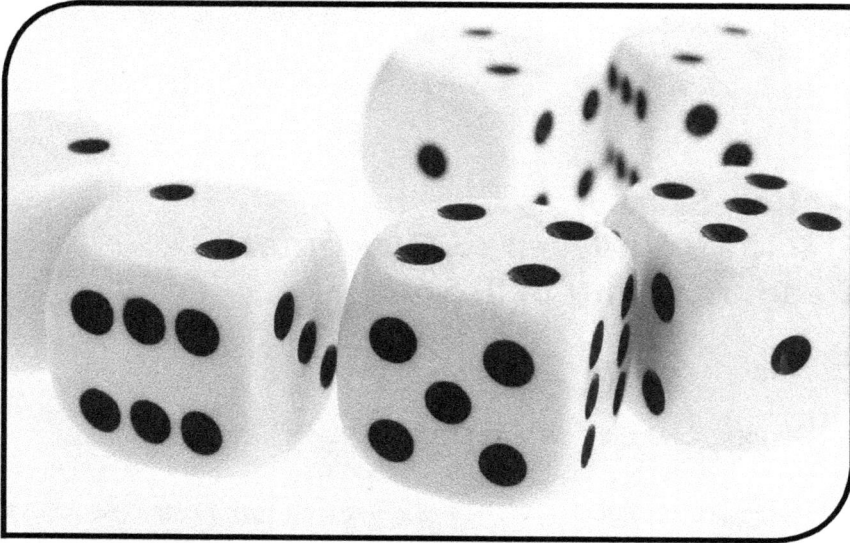

YOUR BRAND MOMENTUM STRATEGY

Jump the Q®'s Momentum Formulae for Success is the process of determining the Why > What > Who > When >Where> How> What if, of your personal brand. By sequentially working through this process you have the ability to get into a highly productive state that can really propel your personal brand and the success you achieve. This strategy allows you to design a personal brand that puts you and your business or career in a highly focused productive zone.

Personal branding is an extremely effective tool because it centralizes all of your business development, career advancement and marketing efforts. Powerful results can be achieved from consistent focus and persistent effort.

This competitive advantage allows your brand to gain the "edge" over its competition and therefore gain amazing momentum.

We all know how productive we are when we are in a flow state. We are in the zone. It's focused positively, results orientated and very satisfying. Imagine being able to access this state of flow for your whole career rather than just for time management purposes from time to time.

Some people jump straight into "how to" build their brand without successfully designing and positioning their personal brand. We see a lot of time and resources wasted when appropriate planning isn't undertaken.

Within the **Brand Yourself Action Plan**, we have captured the specifics of your personal brand as identified in Jump the Q®'s Personal Branding Momentum Formulae for Success. When developing any plan or strategy, the vital ingredients in the Momentum Formulae for Success must be addressed. And we walk our talk here at Jump the Q®. Within the various Action Steps we address the following questions as outlined in the formulae:

- **Why** – why build a personal brand?
- **What** – what is the purpose of my personal brand and what will it achieve? What do I need to have in place to launch or re-position my personal brand?
- **Who** – who do I have to be to have a successful personal brand and who do I need on my team to help me achieve that?
- **When** – when is the best time to launch or re-position my personal brand?
- **Where** – where is my personal brand most visible to my target audience?
- **How** – how will I achieve the objectives of my personal brand?
- **What** if – what if my plans fail, what are my responsibilities that I must cover or protect? What if we are not successful?

All personal brand strategies must be constructed around these specifics. What areas are unclear within your personal brand? The Brand Yourself Action Plan purposefully reviews and responds to these questions and this specific criterion for building personal brand momentum. Within this chapter, we review the resources and future skill set required to meet your personal brand's aims and objectives.

To create a Personal Brand Resource Plan we consider the following:

- your desired outcomes
- your goals
- your business plan
- your preparation
- your command center resources
- your investment
- your network
- your mentor or coach
- your skill set

YOUR DESIRED OUTCOMES

Your outcomes are your personal responsibility. When you are on purpose, provision arrives. Coco Chanel once said, *"How many cares one loses when one decides not to be something but to be someone."* How true!

While you are activating the law of attraction at any given time, even "The Secret" insisted that you determine what you want.

I have often heard the comments "I don't have [this]" or "I don't have [that]" and I question that person more closely with a "Have you ever asked for it? Have you ever considered how you might obtain it?" Or I may ask, "If you could, how would you achieve it?"

Have you declared that something is never going to happen? Henry Ford said, "If you think you can do a thing or have something or think you can't do a thing, or have something – you're right."

There is a school of thought that suggests that your life is exactly what you asked for, with your own free will, your choices, reactions and responses. Obviously, if we don't have the life we would like, than we may need to ask for different things. What are you going to be asking for in the future? Remember the wise words of Maya Angelou, *"You did then what you knew how to do and when you knew better you did better"*. It's never too late to build a better personal brand.

If you take responsibility for yourself you will develop a hunger to accomplish your dreams.

Vision, commitment and faith can make a brand successful. But strategic purpose, planning and preparation will make it great.

Ask yourself these questions:

1. Why build my personal brand? If I had a fantastic personal brand what would I do, be or have?
2. What are my dreams? If I had a magic wand what would I achieve?
3. It is important to me to build a fabulous personal brand because ....
4. What kind of success am I looking for? What precisely do I want for myself and my future?

Determine what resources are necessary to obtain your dreams of success.

We considered these issues within Action Step 3. However, after continuing with the following Action Steps some other goals or wishes may have arisen, so it is timely within this chapter to review your goals and clearly state those goals.

Listen to any voices in your head or suggestions that detract from this positive outcome and write them down on your limitations page to consider at a later time.

YOUR GOALS

Conscious, focused effort is way more dependable than luck in achieving goals.

Henry Ford once said, *"Thinking is the hardest work there is, which is probably the reason why so few engage in it. Obstacles are those frightful things you see when you take your eyes off your goal."* You have to agree that so often we are doing, but not being productive.

Write down any obstacles that come up on your limitations page.

It may be because we haven't set achievable goals, prioritized them and organized a project methodology to achieve them, so we are busy with unproductive tasks. Raymond Aaron, the *One Minute Mentor,* has established an incredible resource for goal setting with his Monthly Mentor program. Raymond advises, *"Forget tasks. Projects and project management are the core skills to develop. Create to-do lists for each project and invest in additional resources to leverage your time. Commit, take action and complete your goals."*

Your personal brand goals, sometimes called objectives, are measurable milestones that lead you to your business goal.

Goals should be S.M.A.R.T.:
    S – Specific about what you want to achieve
    M – Measurable so you can track your progress
    A – Achievable
    R – Relevant to the target market you wish to influence
    T – Time-based, usually a short period of time (no more than a year)

There are three critical steps to developing a successful personal brand strategy.

1.   Determine where you want to take your business
2.   Define the milestones required to get there
3.   Develop the tactics needed to achieve each step

As you work through each of these steps, take the time to reflect on your current activities, decide what worked and what didn't and make adjustments. Determine what resources are necessary to obtain your goals.

If you had all the resources and all the help you needed what would you ask for?

YOUR BUSINESS PLAN

Create a personal brand business plan. A business plan is a formal statement of a set of business or brand goals, the reasons why they are believed attainable, and the plan for reaching those goals. It may also contain background information about the organization or the team attempting to reach those goals.

You can easily develop a business plan from the above goal setting process. Your business plan or goal is your vision of what you want your business to look like in three to five years. It is the guiding light that directs all aspects of your business and enables you to focus in one direction.

YOUR PREPARATION

Your preparation produces payoffs. As Oprah Winfrey said, *"Luck is a matter of preparation meeting opportunity"*. One of the best methods to overcome fear and take advantage of opportunities that may come your way is to anticipate challenges and over-prepare for them. If you are considering leaving your job this may mean budgeting wisely and saving money regularly so you cover start-up expenses and provide your household with your usual contribution.

Part of your preparation may also include asking yourself, "What is the worst thing that could happen?" Confronting your worst fear can be extremely empowering. While life is not a dress rehearsal, preparation pays off.

> Before everything else, getting ready is the secret of success.
> — Henry Ford

There is any number of "how-to" programs available on the market. For example, there are numerous products on how to become a better speaker or how to write an e-Book. Our objective is to assist you prepare for these opportunities and adventures. For example, you can elect to become a speaker and go to platform skills training to improve your performance while on stage.

Our programs and objectives seek to prepare you for the opportunity to speak. For example, have you a bio, head shot photo, overview of presentation, speaker introduction, presentation, presentation handouts or free report, offering, follow up offer, template thank-you email and request for feedback and testimonials email?

Additional information on how to build your professional profile and leverage your personal brand to take advantage of the following strategies, are outlined in the Brand Yourself Resources section.

YOUR COMMAND CENTER RESOURCES

Assess your situation: Consider your available time and resources. Consider your personal preferences. Think about how you might emphasize particular strategies based on your business goals.

One of the best questions to ask yourself is, "If time and money were not an issue, what resources, equipment, systems and staff would I need to fulfill my above goal?"

Who do you need at your Brand Command Centre?

Within this section we consider the "Who" aspect of your Resource Plan. This area is often overlooked. By "Who", I mean: Who will do what? Who do you need in your team? Who will help you fulfill your dreams?

- Define the roles that you would play
- Define the roles that others will play

Write out all the tasks you are doing and also those that need to done.

What tasks should you be doing and which tasks you should be delegating?

What do you need at your Brand Command Centre?

Improving business image and morale is as easy as upgrading the office and workspaces to ensure they appear clean, tidy and professional. This may include new office and reception furniture as well as ensuring vehicles are detailed and re-stocked. I agree with Wally Olins, Founder of Saffron, author of *On Brand*, who sets out the ground rules for business branding when he said, *"Corporate Image ... a company's brand made visible through its people".*

List all the equipment, systems and supplies you will need to build a successful brand.

YOUR INVESTMENT

While you might say "I don't have the money." Look at where are you are spending time, money and effort. Does your personal brand deserve the same investment of resources?

Often the investment is in prioritizing your time to and on your personal success, communicating your needs to family and friends, requesting some support in meeting all of your responsibilities, delegating safely and appropriately some of those responsibilities. It may also mean sacrificing television, gossip magazines, reading or hours surfing the net or hanging out on social media.

It could also mean engaging a cleaner while you focus on your business, requesting your partner or children to take responsibility for certain chores, allocating finances to training and professional development, trading services with other professionals or calling in an outstanding favor.

If you are in full time or part time work and you would like to change jobs or start a new business, start planning now. Decide what you will need to have in place and start working on those things that don't require a lot of money.

If you haven't got the money for business cards and graphic designers, don't worry. Start collecting cards from new contacts and emailing them as follow up, it costs nothing to email. Develop an interesting email signature.

Start working on the content of your website. Write articles in preparation of your Blog posts and Newsletter inserts. Prepare a year's worth of Twitter posts, an email auto-responder series, your speaker bio and presentation.

So much can be done in preparation of your business launch. This type of preparation also means you are out of the gate running. Most people start a business by getting business cards done and going to a networking function and know very little about their industry, products or services.

If you have a dream in your heart, decide to let it out. Maybe you work full time but you have always wanted to be an artist. Start now by planning how you can incorporate it into your life. It may be weekends, it may be after the kids are in bed, may be you have to watch only your favorite programs and not everything in between. Your treasure – that is your focus, time and resources – determines what's truly in your heart. For example, you might say that fitness is very important to you. However, you spend most of your time on the telephone with friends or watching TV. Now, is fitness really the most important thing to you, or your friends or TV?

Where you spend your time reflects your values, that is, what's important to you. We can often be misguided about what's really important to us. If where you are spending your time and resources is not what you would prefer, then change your focus to those things that you would prefer to be a priority.

I agree with Henry Ford's observation, *"That most people get ahead during the time that others waste."*

A professional athlete doesn't achieve their results without investment in lessons, equipment, coaching nor without sacrifice and a certain level of pain. Never stop learning. Learning is a lifelong endeavor.

YOUR NETWORK

Your network is your greatest resource. Network to establish trust, build relationships, generate referrals and leads. You can network your everyday contacts into referral sources and target groups and individuals likely to expand your reach and reputation within your target market. The more you network, and the more distinctive you make yourself, the more you will be remembered and recommended.

Maybe you are not a strong networker, maybe you have a friend or colleague who you could sponsor, and they may be great talkers without the funds to attend various networking functions. Why not pay for them to attend on your behalf? This arrangement can have multiple benefits as your brand has now a third party endorsement and a raving fan. And you didn't have to do a thing other than supply the small cost of the event registration.

You need to make human contacts that generate cooperation and referrals, and you must form a network of people who know you, trust you and respect your business enough to recommend you to prospects when opportunities arise. In short, you need to network.

The most common way people take a measure of who we are is by looking at who we spend time with. They want to find out, first, who we know and, second, how who we know can help them get what they want.

The questions we have to ask ourselves are: Can my network and I help people do things or get things done that they can't accomplish on their own? Can our network solve others' problems?

Become the connector and the consummate problem-solver. A great problem-solver knows everyone. When it comes to building your network – be intentional. Intentionally identify who you want to meet, why you want them and exactly what you hope to get out of the relationship.

It is important to focus your attention on twelve to fifteen contacts that are your best center of influence, which is the people who are well connected. Connect with the connectors or great networkers. If you choose the right people to focus on, you'll have all the time you need to go deep.

Create a list of the top fifty people you know whom you can meet to tell your story. There is only one rule – the person must be able to pull you up in some way via the skills, resources or knowledge that person has. Think strategically. Attempt to meet four people a month to begin with and accelerate as you feel more confident. Always strive to play above your existing game.

Generally, when we discuss networking a number of objections come up as to why you can't spend a majority of your time promoting yourself and what makes you special. List any obstacles that arise as you consider attending various networking events.

YOUR MENTOR OR COACH

You don't know what you don't know. Find a wise mentor who does and who will question you and remained focused on the goal. Find people you would love to work with. Create an A-list of individuals and companies who you believe you could learn from. Who are the top people you would love to have vouch for you? They may be people who already have your clients and are successfully selling to them. Create a list of ten. Do your research on them; introduce yourself, seeking to gain some valuable insight from them.

Alternatively, your mentor list could contain people who are very accomplished at the skills you would like to obtain.

For example, recognizing your need to improve your networking skills you add one of the leading networking gurus to your list and actively pursue a relationship with them. Look for the person who has the job you'd like one day. Look for someone who has qualities you lack and a level of expertise you want to achieve. Look for someone you admire and respect.

You may wish to engage a coach. Coaching that is one-on-one tends to provide the right kind of pressure that makes great leaders from ambitious students.

YOUR SKILL SET

In a sense, your personal brand is made up of these three functions:

1. Performance
2. Communications
3. Presentation

Within this section – Your Skill Set – we consider the issues of your performance as well as your communications skills. In Action Step 6, we dealt with the other issue of your personal brand's presentation.

What skills, training and professional development do you need? As Warren Buffett quite rightly said, "Risk comes from not knowing what you're doing."

Review your skill set in the following areas to determine whether additional training or coaching is required:

- your expertise
- your communications skills
- your conversational ability
- your actions
- your past results
- your self-promotion skills
- your personal growth

YOUR EXPERTISE

Commit to a professional development program in your area of expertise. Some professions such as accountants and lawyers have a legal obligation to maintain their professional development to ensure they remain current with new legislation and practices.

Even a simple half an hour a day will result in you reading over twenty books a year. It is believed that to become an expert on a subject requires as little as five to seven books to be read on the subject. Recognize that while you may not currently be the most knowledgeable in your field it is a simple daily reading program for twelve months that would put you into the top ten percent of your field.

A study has shown that on average we travel over ten thousand miles a year. If you listen to educational audio programs consistently, at the end of three years you have acquired the same level of information required to complete a two year college education.

Once we choose a narrow focus, we need to work to become excellent at it. Do whatever it takes to ensure you have the technical expertise and competence to deliver. Isolate the discipline you want to improve and then find the best resources available to provide you with the greatest impact in the shortest amount of time.

Focus your brand on an area of achievement. The best positioning you can have among your prospects and customers is that of an expert, an authority in your area of expertise. What one area of specialization will be the most helpful to your brand?

YOUR COMMUNICATIONS SKILLS

Effective communication skills are vital to building your personal brand. Five common communications skills that you may need to review include; public speaking, rapport-building skills, asking the right questions, being a good conversationalist and perceptual agility or the ability to calibrate the impact or meaning of the communication.

The public perception of a good communicator is that generally they are smarter people than those who are not as articulate.

For example, when you first started developing your brand you may never have considered that you would be in a public speaking role. As an industry expert, however, you may be called on to give a media interview or speak at your industry's annual conference. If after some training in these areas you felt more confident and others where available to assist you, what do you now feel you could achieve? It could be conducting training or keynote presentations around the globe. Maybe your media training and insight now reveals that your own lifestyle TV program on remodeling old furniture is a distinct possibility. And this further expands your thinking. What skills and resources would you need to achieve this outcome? It's very exciting.

Branding draws people like magnets. If you absolutely revel in your audience and their attention, really thrive on it, you're probably considered very charismatic.

YOUR CONVERSATIONAL ABILITY

Developing a well rounded, multi-dimensional personal brand takes time, long range strategic thinking and commitment. Your personal brand relies heavily on your conversational ability to easily and effort-lessly create meaningful relationships through brief conversations.

Most of our clients are very successful at what they do. They come to us to learn how they can be more influential in mobilizing people for specific purposes. A person's influence is directly proportional to the overall appeal of their personal brand. The more well rounded you are, the more compelling you will be to others.

Following are some areas where you may develop a stance on to expand the appeal of your brand:

- current events
- reading
- politics
- hobbies
- sports
- spiritual/religious affiliations
- participation in charities
- travel
- networking
- business
- science

Create your own list of areas which would be attractive and interesting to be involved with, that support your personal brand. Then develop a plan to build your knowledge or involvement in these areas over the next six months.

Select areas that will support your brand and possibly align to your target audience's areas of interest, too. The more interesting we are, the more we will attract other interesting people to us. Think about whom we value the most in our society: people with interesting stories. The more well rounded we are the more upwardly mobile we will be. Being an engaging conversationalist requires a spirited exchange of well-crafted opinions on the subjects of mutual interest. This also requires us to be able to see and appreciate all points of view in a discussion, especially when there is a conflict of opinion.

Ask yourself if they would pick you. Your boss is taking important clients to lunch. They must decide who of the team to take. It must be someone who is interesting, presentable, knowledgeable, a good conversationalist and well mannered. The person must reflect well on the organization. Would the boss pick you?

Being interesting is hard work. It takes a commitment to ongoing learning, as well as developing the skill of being able to engage others in a meaningful conversation. All it takes to be interesting is to exhibit a basic curiosity about life, people and the world around you. The more we know and the more we are able to enrich others' lives, the more people will want to know us. People have short attention spans. You cannot afford to be boring.

YOUR ACTIONS

Your actions speak louder than words. Create an exhaustive list of all the actions, behaviors and activities you think will help you build your personal brand equity. Then implement them one by one, not starting on a new strategy until the previous one has been fully completed.

Habits are the behaviors we practice unconsciously. We are not born with a certain set of habits. Every single one of our habits is learned behavior. Therefore, we must keep practicing those habits that empower us and unlearn those that have disempowered us.

What are the best positive activities to support your brand? The best way to be described by clients is as a nice person. What do people value? Research into tipping has revealed that larger tips do not co-relate to efficient and prompt service. Instead people tip more when the staff makes them feel good. We pay more for small gestures of friendship.

Consider the following gestures and determine if you can incorporate them into your personal brand:

- show your appreciation
- smile a lot
- be open, honest and direct with others
- write thank-you notes all the time
- send a small gift on important occasions
- express condolences
- always acknowledge birthdays
- send relevant articles to clients and contacts
- congratulate your adversary when they have a win
- be the first to contribute to another's charity
- support event organizers at the functions you attend
- say "Good morning" and "Good night" to everyone
- take your team to lunch
- say "Thank you for a productive day at work."
- give without expectation
- always be early
- have a firm handshake
- make the best of tough situations
- always speak positively of others
- have a consistent dress standard

Pick a few small actions/activities/behaviors that you can consistently execute to strategically accentuate your personal brand. It must be something that distinguishes you. Build your brand edge with a personalized gift that shows you care.

YOUR PAST RESULTS

Success rarely comes easily or by accident, in most cases it involves consistent personal development; lessons learned from painful mistakes, clear personal goals, careful planning, self-promotion, continuing education and consistency of effort. No single area of image can make you successful for the long term, but likewise, awareness alone is not enough — you must take action. I have heard many people say "I know that" but they have never and will never implement the insight and will always wonder why nothing ever changes for them.

Joyce Meyer, in her bestselling book, *Battlefields of the Mind*, states, *"Positive minds produce positive lives. Negative minds produce negative lives. Positive thoughts are always full of hope and faith. Negative thoughts are always full of fear and doubt. Remember Proverbs 23:7 'For as a man thinks in his heart, so he is.' "*

Your challenge is to acknowledge the results of your current thoughts as evidenced in your current life and determine to adjust your thoughts and mindset.

YOUR SELF PROMOTION SKILLS

Because you are your own PR department you must become comfortable with a degree of self promotion to build your personal brand. People need to know who you are and what you do.

There are four major myths of self-promotion. They are:

1. others should talk about my accomplishments, not me
2. if I'm good enough, people will hear about it
3. self-promotion will make me look arrogant
4. you can't control what people think anyway

The myths you believe often mask a deeper insecurity about the value you place on what you have to offer. If you don't fully believe in yourself, you'll naturally resist stepping into the spotlight. This resistance, plus generations of conditioning to be humble and stand on the sidelines, has left many unprepared for today's ultra-competitive business world.

That doesn't mean you have to play the role of a pushy salesperson to get ahead. But it does require taking small steps outside your comfort zone. Get familiar with your strong points. Write them down if necessary and put them somewhere you'll see them often. Practice talking yourself up in front of friends: they'll give you honest feedback about what works and what doesn't.

Most importantly, tap into your passion for what you do. By denying your passion a voice, you keep the world from benefiting from what you have to offer.

If you are sold on your brand and communicate the fact with passion, you'll sell your clients on yourself without selling your soul.

Decide your personal success is worth investing in and that any sacrifices are small in comparison to the rewards. And don't let lack of time or money be an excuse for not starting.

On the other end of the self promotion spectrum are those I call serial self promoters. It is important to remember that there is a thin line between arrogance and confidence and that line is fear. One of the greatest hindrances to building a really great personal brand is aggressive self promotion or some call it professional arrogance. At the heart of this aggressive behavior or arrogance is the genuine fear that we are not good enough, so we try and compensate by projecting that we are more than we actually are. Instead of letting our track record and happy clients build our reputation, we may talk incessantly about how great we are. Instead just be great and let others tell others how great you are. If this could be perceived about you, note it on your limitations page.

A great personal brand also knows when to embrace silence. They are polite, courteous and do not try to dominate conversations. They embrace the rules of social etiquette. They tell people about their impressive accomplishments, but they spend a great deal of time asking questions and showing interest in others. Such people are confident, but they also work hard, letting their actions account for a significant part of their self-promotion. A successful marketer is a nice person who treats all people well.

YOUR PERSONAL GROWTH

Is a skill set or mindset issue hindering your performance? As you continue to refine your brand and purpose … begin to notice when you go off purpose. What have you allowed to happen? It may be a continuing drama, other people's health issues arise, may be your own health deteriorates or your life is suddenly in crisis mode or maybe you choose to rescue someone repeatedly.

Be very careful to look beyond the events. Look for the emotional hooks that may exist here. What emotions arise? What belief of yours is reinforced in this behavior and/or event?

If you believe you have found your purpose and are having difficulty remaining on your path, it may be wise to identify this as a potential area for personal growth. Use a mentor, coach or counselor to help you remain accountable to your purpose and ask the hard questions of why you are allowing life to side track you from your purpose.

Ask yourself, "Who or what am I allowing to take me off purpose?" Add any thoughts to your limitations section in Chapter 10.

> Always, remember that when you take the leap, back-up arrives.
> — Rachel Quilty

Chapter 16

Action Step 9.
Deploy Your Personal Brand Message

Why do some business owners or colleagues make it big while you work eighty-hour weeks and are yet to make it? Why do your competitors with less ability consistently get more business than you do? Why do you never seem to reach your income goals? When does it get easier? Why are you the best kept secret in the market place?

As mentioned previously, research has shown time and again there is a direct correlation between a product's level of awareness and its market share.

Keeping up a consistent flow of information increases your chances of influencing what people think of you, your product, service or company. The absence of such information leaves it for your critics and competitors to define your business.

Almost eighty percent of all sales are made after the fifth contact. Of the one hundred percent of businesses who make that first contact, forty percent make the third, twenty-five percent the fourth, and ten percent the fifth. And the same principles apply to personal branding.

Visibility is more important than ability. In a competitive, fast-moving, global economy, you must be noticed in order to succeed. When working remotely your visibility will decrease. With this in mind, you must ensure that you're communicating your value with every email and every phone call.

Deploying your personal brand message includes considering and developing:

- your compelling brand message
- crafting your brand message
- your testimonials and endorsements
- your customers buying strategies
- your initial contact
- your action taking
- your brand message conveyance
- launching a successful personal brand
- your communication plan

> Action is the foundational key to all success.
>
> — *Pablo Picasso*

Let's look at each of these components of deploying your personal brand message.

YOUR COMPELLING BRAND MESSAGE

Developing a clear personal brand value proposition is perhaps the single most important strategic process in which your brand can engage. A value proposition is a clear statement of the tangible results a customer gets from using your products or services. Part of your Personal Brand Offer Definition also includes the Value Proposition, which is determined when you answer these two questions:

1. What is the Value Proposition to the Customer?
2. What pain are we solving?

Within a sales process this may be your Unique Selling Proposition (USP) or your Unique Value Proposition (UVP). Having a personal brand value proposition is interesting, but what is it and do your customers know why it is important to them? Does your brand have a value proposition that is clear and compelling to your target audience?

If you cannot clearly define the value proposition for your brand, are you making it more difficult to be able to sell your product or service?

A value proposition needs to resonate on your customer's WIIFM – "What's In It For Me?" Answering that question with measurable results will increase your target's interest in what you have to offer. And if you do, you have a much better chance of turning them into a customer.

Your personal brand compelling brand message or personal brand value proposition:

- is a short description of your business that catches your ideal client's attention
- tells them how you can help solve their problem
- conveys what value you bring to the relationship, what makes you different and the benefit they will experience by working with you
- explains why they should trust you and should do business with you rather than your competition, not how do you do it

Your customers only care about what you can do for them and the benefits they will get by investing their money with you. You also need to provide information that your niche or target audience wants.

Find out what questions your market is actually asking by going to this link: http://labs.wordtracker.com/keyword-questions/
Type in your keyword and you will see what people are actually typing into the search engines. This is a vital part of your research when trying to find out what answers your market is looking for and what value can you provide them.

CRAFTING YOUR BRAND MESSAGE

The following checklist is useful when reviewing, building and measuring your Personal <u>Brand</u> Message:

- <u>Specialization:</u> Does it identify your specialty? Is there a message to market-match? Is it an appropriate medium/channel?
- <u>Leadership:</u> Does the message reinforce your position as an authority in your field?
- <u>Attributes:</u> Is the message, medium/communication channel consistent with your brand?
- <u>Distinctiveness:</u> Does the message highlight or portray the distinctive flavor of your brand?
- <u>Visibility:</u> Is your message visual to your target audience?
- <u>Consistent:</u> Is your branding being seen consistently by your target audience?
- <u>Build Relationships:</u> Does your message and medium enter the conversation in your target markets heads? Are you building rapport with your message?

Your brand should be so persuasive that your target market considers no other choice but your brand. To consider the alternative – would be unthinkable! You become the "only choice" brand. Increasing your brand awareness increases your persuasiveness.

In Cialdini's book, *Influence – The Psychology of Persuasion*, he outlines a number of factors that contribute to how people are influenced and in turn logically how you can influence others. The various items addressed could act as a Persuasion Audit for your marketing plan and compelling brand message.

So what is influence? Influence is the ability to get people to do things they don't want to do and like it. We know our personal brand is influential when others take action solely because we did or because we recommended they do.

Another key influential indicator of your personal brand is when others seek out your advice on issues beyond your area of expertise. What this means is that people value you for more than just your knowledge. They have faith in your judgments and instincts.

Within your marketing, do the following elements apply?

- Liking – People like people who are like them. People also like to work with and support those they like. That is why relationships and customer service are so important and why networking is an effective business tool.
- Reciprocity – People are willing to comply with requests from those who have provided something first. Individuals are more likely to give after receiving.
- Social Proof – People are more willing to take a recom- mended action if they see evidence that many others, especially those similar to them, are taking action. The individual's decision confirmed by the social proof of others making the same decision. People like to follow the crowd.
- Consistency – People will act consistent with their previous behavior. If they previously agreed to something, they are more likely to agree to another request.
- Scarcity – We are all hard wired not to want to miss out. The psychology working here is that people are more motivated by fear of loss than the desire for gain.
- Authority – People respect a good communicator to whom they attribute relevant authority or expertise. The trappings of authority are afforded more obedience. We also trust experts to give us good advice.
- Legitimacy – The message must be logical, congruent and valid. People like to know why. Always include a "because" in your communications.
- Contrast – Offering a contrast or highlighting the cost of not acting is very motivational. This may also include possible income outcomes as a result of a small investment in this product or service.

When planning a marketing and/or sales strategy ensure it supports these attributes and recognize the human psyche plays a funda- mental part in your brand's acceptance or non-acceptance.

YOUR TESTIMONIALS AND ENDORSEMENTS

Obtain testimonials from your clients. The perceived importance of your client and their testimonial is very compelling when building your brand ... as is media coverage. Testimonials and your client's caliber give legitimacy to your brand. In the business world that is the equivalent to a celebrity endorsement of your product.

If you have clients who are famous or a celebrity – without breaching any confidentiality agreements and with specific permission – use this in part of your marketing and promotional material.

Create a list of clients, mentors and potential clients who would be willing to endorse you or provide a written or video testimonial. Note how including testimonials supports Cialdini's principle of social proof.

YOUR CUSTOMERS BUYING STRATEGIES

The goal is to make the first impression a powerful statement of the beneficial result the prospective client is going to receive from purchasing your products or services. The only reason they deal with you is that, to some extent, they see an advantage in it for them-selves. They are buying a result or a benefit.

Your personal brand must:

- reach your target clientele
- reinforce your brand and preferred reputation
- generate trust
- have a degree of longevity and consistency

Even though the marketplace is shifting from product to service orientation, from hard products to soft products, customer buying strategies remain the same. Eighty percent of all buyers are visual. Largely we follow the VAK buying strategy.

A visual experience is followed by an auditory thought or comment followed closely by the feeling or kinesthetic experience that it feels right to buy. This means buyers still need to see something in order to help them validate their purchasing decisions. Something must replace the tangible product. And that something is your personal brand and reputation.

What is relevant is the buyer's perception? We must start managing our buyer's perceptions by clarifying and intentionally promoting our personal brand.

When a company is named after a person or builds a personality into its brand, it humanizes an otherwise anonymous corporate entity. Significant evidence exists – that client's buy the person first, followed by the company and products or services and lastly, price.

How much time is spent on focusing on price strategies and pricing structures? Clearly the most effective way to package ourselves is to create a compelling personal brand. Therefore, promote your personal brand, then your business, then the products and services and lastly the price.

Information overload is another compelling reason to why building your personal brand is a must. We are bombarded with information. The best personal brands offer something specific and simple. And present them as the safe choice. People crave clarity.

It has been said that the ability to deliver a single simple point is a lost art. Our experience has been that the personal brand that stands for a single, powerful message wins every time.

It's that unique combination of your best qualities and attributes that your personal brand has to portray – not just when you are there in person, but when you're not there also. When your prospective customer or employer goes to your website, or reviews your resume, or leaves a voice message, you want those accessories that you use in business or professional life to speak clearly and elegantly about who you are.

Your marketing should at all times be:

- goal orientated
- enhancing and
- appropriate

YOUR INITIAL CONTACT

With every new target market interaction there is a method of building rapport quickly that may assist you overcome your concerns about self-promotion. Firstly, you need to create connection with your client. This can be done easily with questions to better understand your client. You need to get permission to do your job, explain your presence through your own credibility statement.

Your client needs to have an expectation of your knowledge, your style and have agreed to get more information about your product or service to allow you to make an offer. All this happens prior to you engaging with your client about your products and services.

Building rapport and creating a credible space to promote your products and service is a science, which is why branding is so important in generating credibility.

TAKING ACTION

Execution! If you are specific and action oriented, your personal brand and your business can really take off. Your personal brand should influence just about everything you do: how you dress, communicate what you do, entertain, network and promote yourself.

If you are passionate about your personal brand, the intensity of your focus and the intentionality of your actions will propel you to levels never imagined.

If you want to make a name for yourself, be the first into action. You can't do this if you get bogged down in over preparation and the pursuit of perfection.

Great leaders make their moves before they are ready. But always, after the strategically planned launch time. In battle, often the enthusiasm to charge in is the most difficult aspect to manage ... waiting for the moment of optimal likelihood of a positive outcome. Often this maneuver would compromise the total campaign. Strategically determine the correct time to enter the competition or battle. Hear the call, "Halt", "Halt" and then proceed when the preparation and strategic time has arrived.

The objective at this stage is to establish ourselves in the mind of our target audience until we achieve "only choice" status. The "only choice" status means that whenever anyone within our target audience thinks of the quality for which we want to be known, we instantly come to mind.

To satisfy this objective, we need to utilize as many creative strategies and tactics as are needed in order to reinforce our personal brand until in our audience's mind we are unquestionably recognized as the only person our target audience thinks of when they think of the word or phrase for which we want to stand.

We know we have reached this elite status with our target market when great people within this audience regularly say great things to other people about you without any prompting. And you know you've hit the jackpot when you attend events and people comment that they've heard great things about you. This is in essence the competitive advantage you are able to generate when you are well branded. Because essentially, we are pre-sold when our good reputation precedes us.

There are three guiding principles to keep in mind when building your personal brand competitive advantage:

- pace yourself
- think small
- be consistent

> In order to create a personal brand, a steady flow of informa-
> tion is needed to raise awareness.   — *Rachel Quilty*

We have this tendency as humans to think that meaningful solutions have to be complicated and difficult. Remember the quote – "Any intelligent fool can make things bigger, more complex, and more violent. It takes a touch of genius – and a lot of courage – to move in the opposite direction." (*Albert Eistein*)

One of the simple ways we build brand equity with our target market is how we maintain contact with our clients. Do your best to show them how much you love them. If we want to outperform the competition, we must be more intentional than they are when it comes to every detail of our business and personal brand.

CONVEY YOUR BRAND MESSAGE

How do you share your passions and broadcast your personal brand successfully? It's all about promoting you.

Build your brand in bits and bytes. You must proactively and continuously position yourself for success. Your credibility, visibility, personality and personal style all make up your brand. Build and nurture your brand and you'll make yourself a must have, can't fail professional and you'll do it without being someone you're not.

We provide a step by step guide to increasing your professional visibility both online and offline.

The first hundred-day plan once reserved for CEOs and Politicians is something you need to bring to every new assignment, and particularly, the launch of your re-positioned brand. You too need to develop your brand building game plan.

Launching your branding assault and keeping your branding campaign alive with effective branding strategies and online branding tools and techniques is essential for brand equity growth. Studies show that the average person has to hear another person's message six to eight times to remember that person.

If we invest the time and effort, we will see how our consistent execution of the small things dramatically enhances our personal brand credibility.

Maintaining your brand awareness is simple using Jump the Q®'s "Learn How to Brand Yourself" program. See more information in our Brand Yourself Resources section.

LAUNCHING A SUCCESSFUL PERSONAL BRAND

On the following pages are a countdown and checklist for a successful launch of your Brand:

Note: When launching a new product/service you would develop a specific Action Plan for that new avenue. This may be defined as brand extension. For example, Jump the Q® promotes three distinct areas of business, Personal Branding services, Professional Image services and Business Etiquette and Protocol services. Each has a different market with a similar but different branding concept attached to each. A subtle variation on our branding allows us to distinguish the service within our suite of services.

The following is a sample of issues that may be considered in the lead up to the final launch of a product.

Week 1	• Develop a specific Brand Yourself Action Plan • Create a list of potential clients and who has your potential clients • Make a list of potential communication channels i.e. articles, Blog post, keynote topic
Week 2	• Prepare design brief for new brand and engage graphic designer • Prepare content of emails, sales letters, articles, blog posts • Prepare Bio and Speaker Introduction for yourself • Have corporate bio photograph taken
Week 3	• Put together portfolio i.e. hardcopy or web-based • Prepare keynote topic summary and presentation • Review first round of logo designs • Prepare Website Design Brief
Week 4	• Commence development of website priority content • approve layouts for business cards, logos, and letterhead • Prepare and schedule pitches to potential clients • Approve brochure layout • Prepare Media Kits for press
Week 5	• Send Press Release with head shots to media • Finalize website priority content • Send email to database announcing the launch • Finalize portfolio and sales brochures • Commence daily analysis of topical and industry issues

Week 6	•	Follow up emails to potential clients
	•	Place follow up calls to the media
	•	All materials printed and delivered
	•	Meet potential clients if scheduled
Week 7	•	Launch! And celebrate ...

Your launch may not be for a business but a plan of action or a new job search. Any launch needs a similar kind of timetable.

YOUR COMMUNICATION PLAN

What is a communication plan? When should it be developed? Where does the information in the plan come from? How do you write one, and why should you bother?

A written communication plan will:

- give your day-to-day work a focus
- help you set priorities
- provide you with a sense of order and control
- protect you against last-minute, seat-of-the-pants communications
- prevent you from feeling overwhelmed, offering instead peace of mind

What Is a Communication Plan?

A communication plan is a written document that describes:

- what you want to accomplish with your communications (your objectives)
- ways in which those objectives can be accomplished (your goals)
- to whom your communications will be addressed (your audiences)
- how you will accomplish your objectives (the tools and timetable), and
- how you will measure the results of your program (evaluation)

Communications include all written, spoken, and electronic interaction with target audiences.

A communication plan encompasses objectives, goals, and tools for all communications, including but not limited to:

- periodic print publications
- online communications
- meeting and conference materials
- media relations and public relations materials
- marketing and sales tools
- legal and legislative documents
- incoming communications, including reception procedures and voice mail
- committee and board communiqués
- corporate identity materials, including letterhead, logo, and envelopes
- surveys
- certificates and awards
- annual reports
- signage
- speeches, and
- invoices

The best time to develop your plan is in conjunction with your annual budgeting or organizational planning process.

How to Develop the Plan
Take the following steps to develop an effective communication plan:

Step 1. Conduct a research-communication audit. Evaluate your current communications.

To conduct your own audit, find out:

- what every staff person is doing in the way of communication
- what each communication activity is designed to achieve, and
- how effective each activity is

To get the answers you need:

- brainstorm with communication staff
- talk to other departments
- interview the chief staff executive
- interview the board
- survey your clients
- host focus groups, and
- query potential clients

Step 2. Define objectives. Armed with information from your audit, define your overall communication objectives – the results you want to achieve.

These might include:

- excellent service to clients
- client loyalty
- centralization of the communication effort
- increased employee teamwork
- improved product delivery
- visibility for your personal brand and the industry or profession it represents, and
- influence on government, media, consumers, and other audiences

Step 3. Define audiences. List all the audiences that your personal brand might contact, attempt to influence, or serve.

Step 4. Define goals. With stated objectives, and considering available human and financial resources, define goals – in other words, a program of work for each objective.

Goals include general programs, products, or services that you will use to achieve stated objectives. For example, if the objective is to improve service, goals might include improved training for the client – service function, special communications directed at new clients, a reference manual for complaints, and ongoing information for clients.

Step 5. Identify tools. Decide what tools will be used to accomplish stated goals.

These tools can be anything from a simple flyer to a glossy magazine. Don't overlook less obvious tools such as posters, report covers, Rolodex cards, and websites. Brainstorm ideas with your staff.

Step 6. Establish a timetable.

Once objectives, goals, audiences, and tools have been identified, quantify the results in a calendar grid that outlines roughly what projects will be accomplished and when. Separate objectives into logical time periods (monthly, weekly, etc.).

Step 7. Evaluate the result. Build into your plan a method for measuring results.

Your evaluation might take the form of:

- a monthly report on work in progress
- formalized department reports for presentation at staff meetings
- periodic briefings, and
- a year-end summary for the annual report

Developing a written communication plan will take effort. Plan on three or four days the first time you do it. Once in place, the written plan will smooth your job all year long, earn you respect from the satisfied customers, help set work priorities, protect you from last-minute demands, and bring a semblance of order to your personal brand communication.

Chapter 17

Action Step 10.
Deliver Your Personal Brand Promise

A brand promise is the statement that you make to customers that identifies what they should expect for all interactions with your people, products, services and company.

There's also an element of longevity associated with the promise. The promise says consistency. Buy the brand tomorrow and the brand promise will again be fulfilled. The promise being fulfilled time after time is what makes loyal customers. I agree with other authors that the brand promise is the essence of the brand delivered.

You want to have an incredibly positive personal brand, and it comes down to your personal performance. You must consistently, persistently deliver on your promise because the brand promise is the most important aspect of a brand.

Standing out, keeping your eyes on being relevant to your customers, making sure what you promise is what you can deliver and letting the market know what's different about you, is all part of brand management.

To ensure you deliver your personal brand promise ... it becomes vital to monitor your brand's performance in relation to the following areas of your brand:

- your customer satisfaction
- your customer touch points
- your human touch
- your nurtured target audience
- your promise delivered
- your reputation
- your goodwill
- your mistakes

Let's consider each of these aspects in turn.

YOUR CUSTOMER SATISFACTION

Basically a successful brand satisfies two masters. The brand's owner or the corporation is one, and the other, the brand's customers. This point highlights an important business fundamental that the purpose of a business is to create a customer.

Schedule once or twice yearly a market survey. Ask what does your target audience think of you? What do I want them to think about? Use performance reviews, online surveys using services such as Survey Monkey® to determine where you stand with your target audience.

Remain loyal to your mission and celebrate your successes and your failures. This also means staying interested in the health and welfare of your brand each and every day, keeping attuned to how it's received, and looking for opportunities to promote it.
Keep in mind that often the most important thing in communication is hearing what isn't said. You may wish to periodically conduct a customer satisfaction survey to determine whether your client's expectations are being met and satisfied.

REVIEW CUSTOMER TOUCH POINTS

Review customer touch points annually. What statement about your personal brand are your customer touch points making? The total "experience" a client has with you and your product or services will determine your brand success.

Consider each issue and what message these items say about your personal, professional and business brand? Improve any areas that may have fallen short of your standards. Successful communication occurs when performance matches the image.

Prioritize areas with the most impact for immediate results. These may include your email and correspondence format, email signature, answering machine message and telephone greeting so as to respond to client queries more effectively. Your physical appearance will also have an immediate result and impact and can be easily and inexpensively be improved.

THE HUMAN TOUCH

Too many brands have forgotten one simple truth – human communication is one of your greatest needs.

Research has shown when businesses lose clients, seventy percent are lost because they do not like the human side of doing business with that organization. Through more effective communication, you can build your human side and your personal brand.

You are chosen because something about you engenders trust and makes your target audience decide to do business with you. Clients choose to work with you. Deliver great customer service. Back-up your brand with great performance.

> "A business absolutely devoted to service will have only one worry about profits. They will be embarrassingly large." — *Henry Ford*

The success of your brand is directly related to your attentiveness to your audience. That connection is what earns brand loyalty. So, how are you connecting with your audience? Review your customer touch points or as Siimon Reynolds describes these touch points, your "Love Marks".

Consider these questions carefully:

- Does your attention and love leave a mark?
- Are you speaking the love languages of your clients?
- Do you really see your audience?
- Do you really listen to your audience?
- Do you have your heart open to your audience?

Tim Sanders uniquely reveals the importance of compassion and love as a point of differentiation which will separate you from your competitors. It's a world where nice, smart people win! And love is the killer app.

Kevin Thomson, author of *Emotional Capital*, over a decade ago predicted, *"Organizations in the future will manage feelings, beliefs, perceptions and values – the asset of emotional capital – as the hidden resources with the power to translate people's knowledge into positive action".* We have arrived.

Love your customers and they will love your brand.

YOUR NURTURED TARGET AUDIENCE

You never know ... how you touch a life. Never underestimate the power of your actions. With one small gesture you can change a person's life. For better or for worse! Many of my clients are going through a process of change. At our deepest level we are vulnerable ... and easily lifted by a caring gesture.

Set aside a day a month to call clients, to check in with your employer or supervisor, to see what's the latest with your colleague, vendors, industry stakeholders, to be remembered by the people who you want to have thinking about you. Make notes on each call and keep a file on all of your important contacts.

Ensure your customers are regularly nurtured with your signature gestures such as a gift, note, card; or by acknowledging important occasions to your clients.

YOUR DELIVERED PROMISE

Often you can contribute significantly by doing just what you promised.

There is no surer way to undermine our personal brand credibility than to fail to deliver on our promises. And certainly we can address the problem as it occurs. What about the future? Is it likely to occur again? Is there a system you can put in place to ensure that issue doesn't arise again? Could an email auto-responder series be activated?

A problem or challenge is an opportunity to improve your business, so ask yourself, "What is the solution to this matter? What could I do or implement to ensure it never happens again?"

YOUR REPUTATION

Your reputation is your most precious commodity. You must be concerned about the way you look and appear to others. You must be concerned about what people say and think about you. Your reputation, your promise, your guarantee or "brand equity" is one of the few resources that you have that gives you a sustainable competitive advantage. Your reputation is an asset to be created, nurtured and used to your advantage.

As stated previously, you are cultivating a strong personal brand until such time as it is a proven personal brand. Creating the kind of personal brand equity necessary to build a reputation that precedes you takes a very, very long time. Be patient and drip-feed your target market. It takes time to have accumulated the kind of personal brand equity to make things happen. But don't equate slow progress with no progress.

YOUR GOODWILL

Tim O'Brien, in *The Power of Personal Branding,* considers the idea of forgiveness of mistakes as a measure of your personal brand good-will. He tells us that *"Goodwill is measured by how willing people are to forgive us when we misstep".* How goodwill can be measured is to the degree that others are prepared to forgive us our mistakes. Generally, we are willing to give people a second chance, but it will rely largely on how they respond to the mistake you made. This psychological aspect of branding is encapsulated in the Halo Effect mentioned earlier.

Monitor your client's willingness to forgive you or not to complain when you fail to deliver to expectation or to an understood agree-ment in quality, timing or substance.

Regularly, we can compromise our brand by over-promising and under-delivering. An example of this is conceding to client's dead-lines or promising to deliver a proposal or quote within an unrealistic timeframe. Stop it. Sometimes this issue can be resolved simply by improving your communication and outline what the client should expect at the initial point of contact.

YOUR MISTAKES

Statistics reveal that seventy percent of customers will never tell you about their concerns ... they just won't come back. And this percentage is even higher in women customers. How can you apologize if you are not even aware that you have offended someone or if there is a grievance? Chances are that unless you have created some goodwill it is unlikely that you will recover from a mistake.

An apology should always be absolutely genuine. When you make a mistake own it. Admit the mistake immediately and sincerely request the person's forgiveness. You will rarely be disappointed by the response.

Have you ever genuinely apologized and the client just wasn't receptive to your apology. Chances are you didn't address the apology in a manner that they accept apologies. Within the book, *The Five Languages of Apology,* Gary Chapman explains that we all have a different way of receiving an apology. Unless you clarify what an apology entails for your clients, you may remain un-forgiven. Ask the question, "What would they like me to do?" The client will tell you exactly what an apology looks like to them. Often the solution is simpler than you think. This means monitoring your client's responsiveness. If you are concerned with the lack of response, contact them again, immediately apologizing. Ask if there is a problem which you can assist them with. Clients will be touched that you care and respond promptly.

PART III

Brand Yourself
for Survival

Chapter 18

Measuring the Success of Your Brand

So by now you have strategically and systematically been working on your personal brand and now want to determine how successful your efforts to build your professional profile have been. Consider each of the following in turn to calculate the level of your personal brand's success:

- your personal brand awareness
- your reputation
- your synonymy with your company
- your return on investment
- your personal brand value
- your personal brand equity
- your turnover
- your brand community
- your brand confidence
- your brand loyalty

Let's look at each in turn to determine the level of success.

YOUR PERSONAL BRAND AWARENESS

Branding and brand awareness become essential to your personal brand's success. The following eight brand elements will assist you build and measure the success of your personal brand. Give your personal brand a rating on a scale of one to ten. Ten being excellent!

1. Are you well known for your area of specialization?
2. Are you a recognized leader in your market place?
3. Does your personal brand have a clear personality?
4. Are there elements of your personal brand which are distinctive?
5. How is your personal brand's visibility?
6. Is your personal brand congruent?
    Does performance = promise?
7. Are you persistent in delivering your brand message?
8. Does your personal brand build rapport and help create relationships?

Review your brand's performance. How did you go? It helps to periodically do a self-assessment. You know better than anyone where your personal brand is not delivering. Focus on areas where your brand could improve for dramatic results.

YOUR REPUTATION

Every brand is challenged to remain differentiated, significant and relevant. Therefore, as tangible differences diminish, the client perception of your personal brand now becomes the key market place differentiator.

Warren Buffett wisely said, *"It takes 20 years to build a reputation and five minutes to ruin it. If you think about that, you'll do things differently"*.

Your reputation or "brand equity" is one of the few resources that you have that gives you a sustainable competitive advantage. Your reputation is an asset to be created, nurtured and used to your advantage. This increased perceived value allows you to premium price your services.

What is your personal brand's reputation? What are people saying about you? Does your personal brand have an incredibly good reputation? Or does it need work?

Chances are that if it didn't perform as well as you would have liked it to you may have under-delivered on brand promise. Your brand promise is better understated than overstated. *"Let people be surprised that it was more than you promised and easier than you said"* as Jim Rohn has said.

YOU'RE SYNONYMOUS WITH YOUR COMPANY

Ask yourself these questions:

- Who do you trust more - corporations or people?
- Who is more likely to listen to you - corporations or people?
- Who is more likely to do the right thing
  – corporations or people?

We believe and trust people far more than corporations. Hence, personal brands are far easier for people to relate to, because they represent real individuals, not company names that could be hiding virtually anything. This is validated in the growing profitability of companies where the CEO has a very public and popular personal brand. CEOs and senior executives who are not developing their own personal brands aligned to their organizations are potentially leaving money on the table.

A frequently asked question is, "Do I develop a company brand separate to my personal brand or make my personal brand my company brand?"

For a business owner your personal brand should be completely aligned and similar in look and feel to your company brand, however you may wish to add an individual twist. For an employee, your personal brand should take precedent over the company brand and simultaneously maintain the company brand values.

Many of the most successful companies use the appeal of a real person to sell the brand name. Many companies play the name game and use celebrity endorsements, third party endorsement or a selected character to promote their product.

Ideally your company brand and personal brand in most circumstances should be one and the same. Your ideal is for your personal brand to be synonymous with your industry and your company, for example Jack Welch, of GE fame, Bill Gates, Microsoft or Warren Buffet, Investor.

A personal brand is more compelling, easy to understand and ultimately more powerful than just a corporate brand. Therefore, measure how closely linked your company brand or industry and personal brand are, as a measure of success.

YOUR RETURN ON INVESTMENT

Sherri Thomas in her *5 Steps to a Powerful Personal Brand* considers a Return On Investment or ROI dashboard to measure and build your success.

This means fully appreciating your target market and gauging which branding channels are the most profitable in terms of connection and investment of resources. Remember Pareto's principle – twenty percent of the activity generates eighty percent of the return.

Create your own ROI Dashboard. What activities are creating the results? Ensure you ask each client how they heard about you and why they chose you?

YOUR PERSONAL BRAND VALUE

Your personal brand is your number one asset! When you can start naming your price and have built significant personal brand equity you know you are becoming a great personal brand.

Regularly monitor and adjust your rates. Measuring your potential brand equity is easy too. Note your current value or worth: $_____/hour. To illustrate brand worth or value we use a simple hourly rate method. You may wish to use annual salary or commission as an indicative measure of success.

Following the completion of your Brand Yourself Action Plan, determine your new or potential personal value or worth: $_____/hour.

If your personal brand worth has increased in actual terms, your personal branding efforts have been successful. If you identified a potential brand hourly rate greater than your current rate, what are you waiting for? Brand yourself today!

YOUR PERSONAL BRAND EQUITY

Has your personal brand worth or value increased? If so you can calculate the financial success of your personal brand in terms of your personal brand equity.

Now subtract your old hourly rate from your new hourly rate and the result is a glimpse of your increasing personal brand equity.

New $_____- Old $_____
= $_____/hour

– Congratulations!!

Your personal brand may not be able to be measured in terms of financial success, but it instead in more interpersonal terms, the quality and number of genuinely valuable relationships you have or in personal terms, how happy you feel about your brand.

YOUR TURNOVER

The most obvious measure of your personal brands success is the improvement in your bottom line. Notice in future years the correlation in improved turnover with focused branding efforts.

> The better your image, the better your bottom line. It's that simple. In thirty seconds your potential client has judged your business and decided whether they like you, whether they trust you and whether they will do business with you. — *Rachel Quilty*

YOUR BRAND COMMUNITY

The measure of your personal brand's success may be seen in a fan club mentality. For example, Demi Moore was able to raise significant donations to a favorite charity using her huge Twitter® account to appeal for aid. You may have thousands of fans on Facebook® who regularly chat with you. Maybe you have a personal Blog that inspires hundreds of comments, or your videos on YouTube® get thousands of viewings.

This community connectivity and reactivity is very valuable and is a great method of measuring the success of your personal brand.

Keith Ferrazzi, Author of *Never Eat Alone*, outlines, *"What distinguishes highly successful people from everyone else is the way they use the power of building genuine relationships – so everyone wins"*. The more genuine supportive relationships you have the greater your brand's success.

YOUR BRAND CONFIDENCE

How do you feel about your brand? Sometimes the only accurate measure of success we may have about our brand is that we feel confident that it is achieving results. Branding takes time.

YOUR BRAND LOYALTY

Your brand must have longevity. Be an evolutionary brand. We can't just forget about our customers once we've established who they are. We have to always be looking at our brand and at our audience and asking, "Is this still working?" and regularly ask "How are we going?" and assess that we are still satisfying our target audience.

Ask yourself these questions:

- Have I lost any customers lately?
- Does the client always seem happy to see me or hear from me?
- How is my target audience?
- And what does my audience think and feel about me?

If your clients and target audience remain happy with your products, services and customer services on an ongoing basis your personal brand has established a significant level of success. Congratulations!

Generally, you are the human touch of your personal brand. You control the message. Your enthusiasm, passion and commitment will inspire.

A clear measure of your brand's success is your target audience and client's loyalty to your brand. When you have loyal followers who respond to your recommendations then you can be confident that you have created a very successful personal brand.

Chapter 19

Your Brand Success

Personal branding is the most powerful success and business building tool ever developed. You have now learnt how to create a game plan that builds visibility and credibility by making yourself the authority personal brand in your industry as well as an indispensable resource to a tightly targeted group of your best potential clients and customers. Congratulations!

At the very heart of personal branding is defining who you really are. This means that to build a strong brand requires a clear understanding of your true authentic self. Your personal brand is shaped by your core values, passions, personal characteristics or traits, unique and signature talents, accomplishments and your goals.

This is the surprising aspect of personal branding that most people don't appreciate until they start the journey. Personal branding is about discovering and designing the very best you. If for no other reason than these ... branding yourself for success is imperative.

The strength of your brand is fuelled by how others perceive you. The devotion of your target audience is essential to realizing your goals and dreams.

You don't have to have a personal brand that commands the attention of the national press or the world stage in order to inspire people to have a powerful, positive feeling about you.

All you need to do is develop a **Brand Yourself Action Plan**. Review these steps over and over to build a persuasive personal brand and dominate your marketplace.

Action Step 1.   Discover your existing personal brand
Action Step 2.   Determine your brand's target audience
Action Step 3.   Define your true personal brand
Action Step 4.   Dominate your marketplace as the authority
Action Step 5.   Design your unique personal brand
Action Step 6.   Develop your brand's signature style
Action Step 7.   Devise your personal brand marketing plan
Action Step 8.   Decide your desired outcomes, resources and skill set
Action Step 9.   Deploy your personal brand message
Action Step 10. Deliver your personal brand promise

Now you know why some people seem able to attract clients and customers by magic. Their marketing seems effortless. Everyone knows their name, and they get all the business they can handle. No longer will you be wondering, "What's their secret? What makes them so attractive and compelling?"

Keep these ten rules firmly in place as you move your personal brand forward.

1. Be true to your brand and yourself
2. Get to work early
3. Do your homework
4. Have a good attitude
5. Have an opinion
6. Do it faster
7. Communicate more than others
8. Over deliver on your promises
9. Play with integrity
10. Surround yourself with supporters

Personal branding allows you to take control of your identity, and influence the impression that people have of you, which helps you accomplish any number of the following:

- build a powerful personal brand
- create a brand that attracts clients
- develop a personal brand that reflects your potential and goals
- premium price yourself through differentiation
- brand yourself an industry-thought leader
- accelerate your career success
- position yourself as the authority in your marketplace
- dominate your niche, and
- become a celebrity in your own field

In essence, your personal brand means:

- being true to yourself
- fulfilling your dreams
- living your dream lifestyle
- following your true purpose
- owning your dream
- narrowing your focus
- discovering your true worth
- prizing your value
- being of service

Your financial success and celebrity status with your target audience are greatly influenced by how compelling your personal brand is. You are now branding yourself for success. Success means different things for different people. However, it is always a process of self-actualization. The process of branding allows you to become the person you were meant to be. Branding makes you an active partner in fulfilling your destiny in business and in life.

The super successful people in this world have had big dreams. They were conscious of the skills, contacts, and hard work that would be needed to achieve that dream and created a plan. And then they worked their plan.

The successful personal brand has the right mix of confidence, passion, likeability, determination, and focus. When you look at successful business leaders, you realize that each has a self-purpose, a call to action and a desire to win.

Improving your image is an investment in building your personal profile, reputation and the results you will achieve. If you want to be a mini celebrity in your field, you must establish a commitment about building your personal brand equity that borders on obsession.

You have arrived!

BRAND YOURSELF RESOURCES

Consider these questions:

- Why do some business owners or colleagues make it big while you work eighty hour weeks and are yet to make it?
- Why do your competitors with less ability consistently get more business than you do?
- Why do you never seem to reach your income goals?
- When does it get easier?
- Why you are the best kept secret in the market place?

Some business owners seem able to attract clients and customers as if by magic. Their marketing seems effortless. Everyone knows their name, and they get all the business they can handle. What's their secret? What makes them so attractive and compelling?

If you want to join them and enjoy this success, you need to ask yourself these questions:

- Do the right people fully understand what you do?
- Have you targeted your most likely customers and delivered a message that speaks to their unique needs?
- Do you struggle to differentiate yourself from competitors?
- When a local paper or trade journal does a story on your area of expertise, do they call you?

The only difference between you and that person is the other person knows how to brand themselves. You too can learn how to brand yourself!

Research has shown time and again there is a direct correlation between a product's level of awareness and its market share. Even more fascinating is the fairly common perception that a better known product is a better product; whether it is or not.

In order to create perceptions, a steady flow of information is needed to raise awareness. Remember your goal is to control the flow of information about you and to do that, you must provide information that clearly defines your business which in turn is you!

So how do you do that?

Jump the Q®, assists clients to build a powerful personal brand by guiding them through the following processes:

- Create your personal brand – complete our **Brand Yourself Action Plan**
- Dominate your Niche – Join our "How to Brand Yourself" program. The Ultimate Training Resource for Branding and Marketing Yourself
- Position your personal brand – complete the brand yourself the authority or brand yourself a celebrity program

Congratulations!

NEXT STEP

Step 1.   Create your personal brand by completing our step by step Brand Yourself Action Plan.

By now you should have an excellent grasp of your preferred personal brand, areas of improvement to build on as you become known for your passion and expertise.

The next step is designed to assist you create and build your personal brand and leverage your professional profile towards becoming an authority in your industry – that is … complete the 'Brand Yourself Action Plan'.

Here's a taste of what you'll learn inside this amazing brand yourself action plan:

- The **ten Principles to positioning your Personal Branding** in detail so you Brand Yourself the Industry Leader …
- The number one branding mistake that you cannot ignore, if you have even half a chance of **succeeding as the industry expert** …
- How we stumbled upon the **eight laws to building a powerful personal brand**, and how it turned upside down almost everything we have been taught to do …
- Why not employing the **four steps to an effective personal brand** could cause your career to crash and burn, never to recover …
- How with **nine steps you can design a simple and effective personal brand** which leverages your professional profile and become a mini-celebrity in your industry …
- How one simple mistake made by most professionals could mean you will never make an extra cent, unless you **ask yourself these three simple questions** …

- **The WOW factor** for professionals and how ignoring this means your career is destined to mediocrity and your bank account to be empty ...
- How a new way to build your network through video, email and blogging can fast track your professional success and **build a network of raving fans** quicker than you thought possible ...
- Why personal branding is one of the laziest ways to wealth, provided you know how and **where to leverage every scrap of effort you make** ...

And much ... much ... more ...

For your personal branding success start your Brand Yourself Action Plan today! For more information ...

Go to http://www.BrandYourselfActionPlan.com

The next steps to building a powerful personal brand include:

Step 2. Dominate Your Niche - Join our "Learn How to Brand Yourself" program. The Ultimate Training Resource for Branding and Marketing Yourself.

Go to http://www.learnhowtobrandyourself.com

Step 3. Step 3. Position Your Personal Brand – complete the Brand Yourself the Authority or Brand Yourself a Celebrity program. Be prepared to say yes to opportunities.

Go to http://www.BrandYourselftheAuthority.com

BONUS OFFER

To measurably improve your
professional image,
personal brand and brand equity,
get your **FREE** Quick Start Guide -
Brand Yourself Blueprint at

www.brandyourselfbook.com

**SEE BELOW FOR FURTHER INFORMATION
ON BRANDING YOURSELF!**

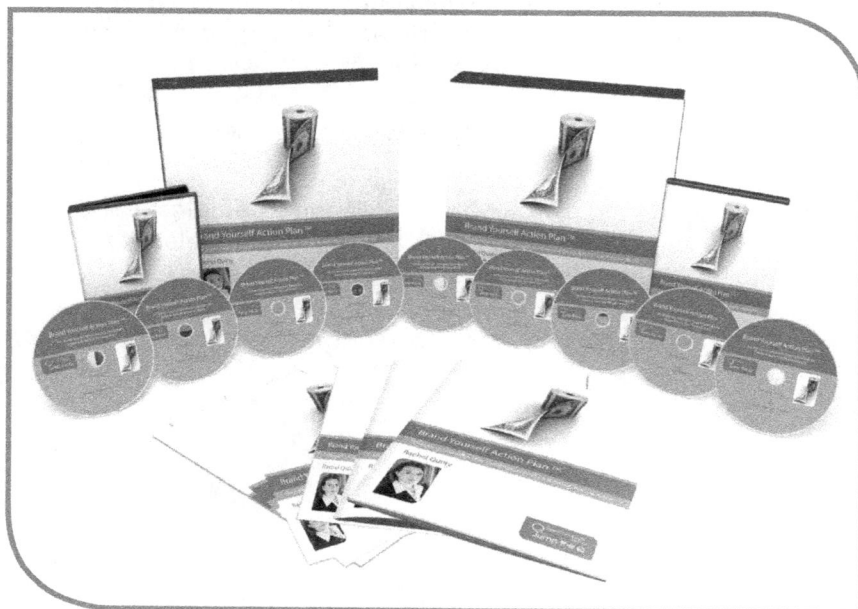

ADDITIONAL RESOURCES AVAILABLE:

Start building your professional profile and leveraging your personal brand to become an authority in your industry with your new **'Brand Yourself Action Plan'.**

See http://brandyourselfactionplan.com for further information.
Go to http://www.brandyourselfforsuccess.com
for additional resources and recommended reading list.

DOMINATE YOUR NICHE

Dominate your Niche – Join our "Learn How to Brand Yourself" Program, the Ultimate Training Resource for Branding and Marketing Yourself.
Go to http://www.learnhowtobrandyourself.com

Position Your Personal Brand – Complete the Brand Yourself the Authority, Brand Yourself an Industry Leader or Brand Yourself a Celebrity programs. Be prepared to say yes to opportunities.
Go to http://www.BrandYourselftheAuthority.com
Go to http://www.BrandYourselfanIndustryLeader.com
Go to http://www.BrandYourselfaCelebrity.com
Go to http://www.BrandYourselfaProfessional.com

SIGNATURE STYLES:

Ladies, create Your Own Signature Style:
Learn the best styles for your body shape.
See http://www.yourownsignaturestyle.com for further information.

Gents, create Your Own Signature Look:
Learn the best styles for your physique.
See http://www.yourownsignaturelook.com for further information.

Ladies, create Your Own Professional Style:
Learn the best professional styles for your body shape.
See http://www.yourownprofessionalstyle.com for further information.

SIGNATURE COLORS:

Ladies, discover Your Own Signature Color:
Discover your best personal colors.
See http://www.yourownsignaturecolor.com for further information.

Gents, discover Your Own Power Color:
Discover your best personal colors.
See http://www.yourownpowercolor.com for further information.

UPDATE YOUR IMAGE: DEVELOP YOUR SIGNATURE LOOK

Ladies, update your image and look stylish with our My Signature Style Club membership. Explore your style, create the best looks for your figure, learn how to coordinate a new wardrobe for yourself, and create a distinctive signature style. Email info@jumptheq.com.au for more information.

ETIQUETTE: BRAND YOURSELF AS ROYALTY

With our business and social Etiquette e-Classes you'll be able to hold your head high and act accordingly in any company with our weekly etiquette lessons.

Email info@jumptheq.com.au for more information.

About the Author

Rachel Quilty, Personal Brand Strategist, Speaker and Author believes, "Building your celebrity profile is as simple as creating a strong personal brand, leveraging your professional profile and developing a signature style to market yourself and stand out from the crowd".

A great personal brand strengthens your message, your personal power and persuasiveness. Personal success relies largely on your ability to communicate ... you can express your potential quietly and effectively without saying a word.

Rachel Quilty has been featured in broadcast media and is frequently asked by journalists to comment on today's most fascinating personal brands, including: Victoria Beckham, Madonna, Paris Hilton, Steve Irwin, Richard Branson, David Beckham and Donald Trump.

Rachel Quilty's tips and strategies have been featured on the Today show, national radio as well as in popular magazines such as Cosmopolitan, Marie Claire, Frankie, Australian Women's Health and Grazia, and most major Australian newspapers. She is also regularly featured within the Working Women and popular Brisbane Circle Magazines.

Rachel Quilty is also the author of a number of Manuals and e-Books and regularly contributes to various business publications, magazines, Blogs and Fashion Forums. Rachel has a keen interest in personal branding, signature styles, business etiquette and professional image.

And this year she releases the first in the Brand Yourself Signature series, "Brand Yourself" available on Amazon.

Rachel Quilty has been invited to contribute to a number of books such as Robyn Henderson's *"How to run a successful business from home and stay sane!"* released in October 2007, and Debbie Mayo-Smith's 2008 book, *"101 Quick Tips – Create a Great Customer Experience"*.

Rachel Quilty highlights, *"Becoming your own unique brand is essential!"* As Judy Garland said, *"Always be a first rate version of yourself instead of a second rate version of someone else"*. Your leading attribute is your personal image. What people see is what they expect to get.

The best personal brand is determined more by what your audience or clients expect to see, and what positions you favorably in their mind, than just looking professional. What is your signature style and what will brand you as professional, individual and credible?

Author's note: We'd love to hear from you. What worked, what didn't, what was your experience, what were your outcomes? Please feel free to email us, especially with your personal branding success stories. We love to share them with our other clients as inspiration and a guiding light. Our contact information is on the followin page.

Look after yourself and your success!

Many regards,

Rachel Quilty
Your Personal Brand Strategist @ Jump the Q Inc.
'The Authority' on Personal Branding

About Jump the Q®

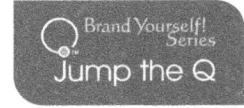

Our vision
The premier strategic personal brand management institution globally

Our mission
To nurture dreams of success through intensive informational and experiential learning courses, seminars and workshops; focused on education and providing valuable content to build and leverage your personal and professional profile; and brand yourself the authority in your industry.

Our mission statement
To assist you to develop a unique personal brand and professional image that reflects your potential and your aspirations through education and encouragement.

Our Philosophy
As a dedicated personal branding firm, our emphasis is on providing clients with a professional edge and a credible image. It is our belief that if you look and act successful you will be. Success increases your quality of life, your sphere of influence and your ability to make a positive difference in your own life and that of others.

You can contact us as follows:

United States Office	Australian Office
7477 W. Lake Mead Blvd., Suite 170	607 Ipswich Rd
Las Vegas, Nevada, 89128	Annerley QLD 4103
PO Box 28909	Australia
Las Vegas, Nevada 89126	
United States	
Email: info@jumptheq.com.au	Email: info@jumptheq.com.au
Bus: + 1(702) 367 7373	Int Bus: +61 7 3848 8777
Fax: + 1 (702) 220 6444	Ph: 1300 655 755 (within Australia)
Web: www.jumptheq.co	Web: www.jumptheq.com.au

www.ingramcontent.com/pod-product-compliance
Lightning Source LLC
Chambersburg PA
CBHW051206200326
41519CB00025B/7019